Samsung Galaxy S24 Ultra User's Manual

A Comprehensive Step-by-Step Guide with Useful Tips & Tricks to Master the Samsung Galaxy S24 Ultra New Features and Latest Android 14 Updates

Perry
Hoover

Copyright © 2024 Perry Hoover

All rights reserved.

It is not legal to reproduce, duplicate, or transmit any part of this document by either electronic means or in printed format. Recording of this publication is strictly prohibited

Disclaimer

The information in this book is based on personal experience and anecdotal evidence. Although the author has made every attempt to achieve an accuracy of the information gathered in this book, they make no representation or warranties concerning the accuracy or completeness of the contents of this book. Your circumstances may not be suited to some illustrations in this book.

The author disclaims any liability arising directly or indirectly from the use of this book. Readers are encouraged to seek Medical. Accounting, legal, or professional help when required.

This guide is for informational purposes only, and the author does not accept any responsibilities for any liabilities resulting from the use of this information. While every attempt has been made to verify the information provided here, the author cannot assume any responsibility for errors, inaccuracies or omission.

Printed in the United States of America

Table of Contents

INTRODUCTION i
CHAPTER ONE 1
New Features 1
    Design and colors 4
    AI features 9
    Battery life and charging 24
    Software and support 28
CHAPTER TWO 35
Setting up your device 35
    How to turn on your device and set it up 35
    How to set up your device with Fast Pair 40
    How to insert the SIM card 45
    How to transfer photos to your computer 47
CHAPTER THREE 50
Set up eSIM on your S24 Ultra 50
    Benefits of using eSIM on your S24 Ultra device 51
    Understanding the prerequisites for setting up eSIM ... 52
CHAPTER FOUR 62
Message Delivery Report 62

How to turn on Message delivery on your S24 Ultra device 62

How do I know if a text message was received 64

How do I know someone ignores my text message 66

How to find out if your number is blocked 67

How to change text notification sound 69

Google Messages App 73

CHAPTER FIVE 75

Camera Feature 75

Understanding the Camera Feature 76

Camera settings for capturing Photos 82

Advanced camera settings for capturing videos 85

Tips and tricks for capturing stunning Photos 88

Tips and tricks for capturing stunning videos 90

How to edit photos and videos on your S24 Ultra 92

How to share photos and videos on Social Media 93

Accessories to enhance your S24 Ultra Camera experience 95

CHAPTER SIX 97

Object Eraser on your S24 Ultra 97

What is Object Eraser Feature 97

How to use Object Eraser to remove unwanted objects from images 99

Benefits of using this feature 101
CHAPTER SEVEN 104
Pairing Earbuds 104
    How to use the Galaxy Wearable app to pair Earbuds to your new device 105
    Troubleshooting common pairing issues 108
    How to optimize your Earbud experience 110
CHAPTER EIGHT 113
Wi-Fi Calling Feature 113
    How to use Wi-Fi calling 116
CHAPTER NINE 121
Battery Life 121
    How to extend the battery life on your S24 Ultra device 123
CHAPTER TEN 126
Multitasking 126
    Benefits of Split-screen Multitasking 128
    How to enable Split-screen on your S24 Ultra device 130
    How to customize Split-screen layouts 132
    Troubleshooting Split-screen issues 134
CHAPTER ELEVEN 138
Developer options 138

How to turn on developer options on your S24 Ultra device 139

The benefits of turning on Developer Mode 141

CHAPTER TWELVE 147

Creating GIF on your S24 Ultra 147

How to create GIF from Photos in Gallery 147

How to take Burst shot and create GIF with this feature 149

How to use the Camera app to create GIF 150

CHAPTER THIRTEEN 152

Outlook Email 152

What is an Outlook Email 152

How to set up this feature on your S24 Ultra 153

Benefits of using Outlook 154

CHAPTER FOURTEEN 158

Tips and tricks on using your S24 Ultra device 158

Twenty-One Best Tips and tricks for your S24 Ultra device 159

CHAPTER FIFTEEN 216

Android 14 new updates with S24 Ultra 216

What is Samsung Android Update? 217

How to Update Android 14 (One UI 6.0) on Samsung Galaxy S24 Ultra 218

How to Update Android 14 (One UI 6.0) on Samsung Galaxy S24 Ultra using Odin 221

CHAPTER SIXTEEN 229

Considering an Upgrade: Samsung Galaxy S24 Ultra vs. S23 Ultra 229

Galaxy S24 Ultra vs. S23 Ultra: design 230

Galaxy S24 Ultra vs. S23 Ultra: display 234

Galaxy S24 Ultra vs. S23 Ultra: performance 237

Galaxy S24 Ultra vs. S23 Ultra: battery and charging 241

Galaxy S24 Ultra vs. S23 Ultra: cameras 243

Galaxy S24 Ultra vs. S23 Ultra: software and updates 247

CHAPTER SEVENTEEN 254

Troubleshooting 254

Common troubleshooting issues and solutions 256

CONCLUSION 281

ABOUT THE AUTHOR 283

INTRODUCTION

If you were to make a list of the features that you would like to see in the perfect mobile device, you would certainly end up with the Galaxy S24 Ultra as the gadget that best meets your needs. The Samsung S24 Ultra appears to be operating from the same checklist as its competitors, and it is prepared to impress fans and enthusiasts alike. The Galaxy S24 Ultra emerges as the leading pick independent of price, which is a surprising revelation given the multiple qualities it possesses.

Looking for a battery life that is truly exceptional? Even when subjected to heavy use, the Galaxy S24 Ultra is able to last for more than a day, surpassing even the greatest smartphones and having outlasted all prior Galaxy models.

Are you also looking for camera capabilities that are unmatched? The Galaxy S24 Ultra surpasses its predecessors by producing photos that is of a higher quality, despite the fact that the specifications may indicate otherwise. When it comes to taking a wide variety of photographs, it continues to be the most adaptable alternative. You will consistently be able to take better photographs with the Galaxy S24 Ultra.

Then what else do you require? Those who are passionate about gaming will find that the Galaxy S24 Ultra is among the best gaming phones that have ever been produced. It outperforms even the most powerful Android gaming smartphones and has the potential to match or perhaps surpass the lightning-fast performance of the best smartphones currently in the market.

In the case of professionals who rely on their mobile devices for business, the S24 Ultra provides features that are superior to those offered by the best smartphones you can find currently in the market. One of these features is the Samsung DeX software, which can turn your mobile device into a virtual laptop complete with windows and an application dock.

The Galaxy S24 Ultra demonstrates Samsung's apparent dedication to breaking new ground in the smartphone industry. Nevertheless, despite its many achievements, it is impossible to ignore the things that it is lacking: elegance and simplicity.

Although this is the case, the Galaxy S24 Ultra continues to be an outstanding option. The long-lasting battery life, amazing cameras, and the indispensable S Pen make it a gadget that stands out from the crowd, despite the unsatisfactory software and artificial intelligence elements that are unnecessary. For the purpose of maximizing my productivity, I rely on this phone rather than my laptop or tablet because it provides unparalleled power and convenience. This is the item that I proudly display to represent the future of technology; it is a device that enables me to accomplish everything with the least amount of weight and the most amount of capabilities.

CHAPTER ONE

New Features

Samsung's Galaxy S24 Ultra pushes the boundaries of what it means to be ultra, breaking through the boundaries of the smartphone category with its features that are unmatched. This device is superior to its predecessor in every way; it has a longer battery life, improved performance, and photographic capabilities that are even more advanced than those of its predecessor. It is highly worth it to invest in the upgrades, notwithstanding that they come with a small price increase.

Nevertheless, the new artificial intelligence features, despite their amazing nature, have the potential to slow down the pace of the phone. This problem is made worse by Samsung's antiquated software, which has a tendency to bury interesting features beneath layers of settings and menus. In spite of this, the Ultra's price tag is justified when one sees it in action, since it possesses some qualities that are tantalizingly close to being miraculous. At the pinnacle of the industry, however, there is still a significant amount of room for more improvements.

Specs

- Dimensions: 162.3 x 79.0 x 8.6mm
- Battery Capacity: 5,000mAh
- Charging: 45W wired, 15W wireless
- Weight: 232g

- Screen: 6.8-inch Dynamic AMOLED 2X, with a peak brightness of 2,600 nits
- Resolution: QHD+
- CPU: Qualcomm Snapdragon 8 Gen 3 for Galaxy
- RAM: 12GB
- Storage Options: 256GB / 512GB / 1TB
- Operating System: Android 14 with One UI 6, providing 7 years of upgrades
- Rear Cameras: 200MP wide (f/1.7), 12MP ultra-wide (f/2.2), 50MP periscope (f/3.4, 5x optical zoom), 10MP telephoto (f/2.4, 3x optical zoom
- Front Camera: 12MP (f/2.2
- Refresh rate: Variable from 1Hz to 120Hz
- Colors Available: Titanium Violet, Titanium Gray, Titanium Black, Titanium Yellow, Titanium Blue, Titanium Green, and Titanium Orange

Design and colors

While the Galaxy S24 Ultra is strikingly similar to its predecessor, the Galaxy S23 Ultra, there are some modifications that, at first glance, would appear to be entirely insignificant. Regardless of some distinctive variations, such as the speaker grills and the positioning of the microphone, the overall appearance is mostly comparable. In spite of Samsung's commitment to perfection, the design does not strike an immediate chord with the audience.

However, upon deeper inspection, one discovers certain noteworthy particulars. The back glass is adorned with many layers of metallic paint, which gives it an alluring depth, particularly in the sophisticated natural gray titanium finish. From a personal standpoint, I believe the violet finish to be very striking because it provides a strong contrast to the otherwise polished metal.

The colors, materials, and finishes that Samsung chooses to use are all examples of the rigorous attention to detail that Samsung shows. Each color version has a frame that is softly colored and matches the new Gorilla Glass Armor back. Some of the color options, such as titanium black, maintain an all-black appearance, while others introduce frame tones that are warmer.

In contrast to Apple, which places a strong emphasis on symmetry in its design, Samsung places a greater emphasis on functionality. As a result of the Power and Volume buttons being located on the same side, I am able to reduce the number of unintentional screenshots that occur when I am handling the phone.

Although Samsung, like Apple, has chosen to use a titanium frame for this year's iPhone, the difference between the two is not as noticeable as it is with my iPhone 15 Pro Max. In contrast to the Galaxy Ultra, which is only marginally lighter, the Pro Max has undergone a major weight reduction this year.

It is crucial for individuals who are not familiar with the Ultra series to experience it personally, particularly the delightful click of the S Pen. The S Pen is a multipurpose attachment that can be used as both a motion-sensing stylus and a Bluetooth camera remote, despite the fact that its click mechanism appears to be unneeded because it is not necessary.

In addition, the S Pen provides a level of precision that is comparable to that of professional drawing tools, which sets it apart from the normal rubber-tipped styluses. As a result of its Bluetooth capabilities, it can also be used as a remote control for a variety of phone functionalities, including the camera, which is a functionality that is often available in accessories that are specifically designed for cameras.

As opposed to its predecessors, the Galaxy S24 Ultra features a flat design, which means that it does not have the curved screens that were characteristic of earlier generations. On the other hand, the

Galaxy S24 Ultra has sharper edges, which, although not uncomfortable, give it a considerably larger presence. This is in contrast to the Galaxy S23 Ultra, which had gently rounded curves that made it easy to hold.

Display

The display of the Galaxy S24 Ultra is genuinely remarkable, and it lives up to the high expectations that are placed on a flagship smartphone for its display. It is especially impressive when the Vivid color tone option is utilized because it has a screen that is both big and colorful.

A variety of adaptability capabilities, including as adaptive brightness and color tones, are included in this display. These functions evaluate the lighting conditions in the surrounding environment and adjust the visual experience accordingly. The display is capable of achieving an astonishing 2,600 nits of brightness in bright outdoor situations. Although it may not be the brightest display that is currently available, it surely surpasses any potential practical requirement.

The Extra Dim feature is particularly noteworthy since it enables the Galaxy S24 Ultra to maintain accurate color representation even at extremely low brightness settings, which can be as low as one nit. This level of dimness makes it possible to observe something in a discrete manner, such as reading messages while watching a clip; nevertheless, utilizing it so frequently that it becomes thoughtless could be called rude.

Samsung continues to support its one-of-a-kind S-View covers, which provide a small window for displaying critical information such as time, weather, and notifications through a wallet cover case. Although the smartphone does offer an always-on display mode, Samsung continues to support its S-View cases. This distinguishing characteristic has maintained its popularity throughout the course of time, despite the fact that it may not have been in the forefront recently.

AI features

With OneUI 6.1, which is based on Android 14, the S24 series comes standard. The performance is comparable to that of usual Samsung phones. It is packed with a plethora of features and customization possibilities, and Samsung's animations are more fluid than they were in the past. However, this year's software experience is primarily focused on generative artificial intelligence, which is integrated into a number of different parts of OneUI. Without further ado, let's go through each of them in turn.

- **Call Assist**

The name of this feature suggests that it is helpful for making phone calls. You will see a button on the screen that is titled "Call Assist" while you are on a phone call. Tapping this button will allow you to transcribe the call, which will allow you to read what the other person is saying in real time. You also have the option of performing real-time two-way live interpretation, which currently supports thirteen different languages. For instance, I am able to communicate in Chinese, and the digital voice assistant that Samsung provides would automatically play a different language to the other person (which might be anything from Thai to German).

In the event that the other person responds in their language, I will hear the voice assistance in Chinese. Without the need for the internet, this is accomplished on the device itself, and the amount of time that passes between the time that I complete speaking and the other party receiving the translated message is only around three to six seconds, making it a speed that is suitable for use in situations that occur in the real world.

- **On-device translation across several apps**

Additionally, the S24 phones are able to swiftly translate sections of text into another language without the need for the internet. This capability is in addition to the ability to understand phone calls. This is applicable to text that you come across (such as an article on the internet or even an Instagram image that is written in a foreign language) as well as words that you input. Nevertheless, the latter is dependent on the Samsung keyboard. You will see an artificial intelligence button that can immediately convert the text you are typing into a different language if you are using Samsung's first-party keyboard.

- **Circle to search**

Rather than being a function that is exclusive to Samsung, this one is a Google feature. To put it simply, you can quickly conduct a Google Lens search by circling or scribbling over any region of the screen. A line of text in a photograph can be highlighted and translated in a short amount of time, and I can also look up a piece of clothing that someone is wearing when I do this. The results of the search are really precise, and they frequently display the thing that I am seeking for.

My experience with it has been quite beneficial. It was possible for me to translate a Japanese caption in order to understand what she was saying.

- **Generative AI photo editing**

The native photo gallery on the S24 phone is capable of doing generative artificial intelligence photo editing, which means that it can replace current pixels with ones that are completely unique.

Following the Google Pixel 8 series, the S24 phones are the second smartphones to perform this natively on-device, and in certain respects, Samsung's artificial intelligence is superior to that of Google's. Since the generative process can take anywhere from five to twenty seconds, it has been a time-consuming procedure for me in the past when I wanted to make multiple modifications on a Pixel 8 phone. The S24 phones are capable of completing this operation more quickly.

In order to maintain the image's realistic appearance, I frequently make use of this function to remove something from an image and then employ generative artificial intelligence to fill in the missing portions.

Cameras

It was the Galaxy S23 Ultra that reigned as our top camera phone overall in the previous year, so when reports began to circulate that Samsung could cut the optical zoom from 10x to 5x, it caused significant alarm. Alongside its 200-megapixel sensor, dual zoom lenses, 100-times digital astrophotography, artificial intelligence image upgrades, and other capabilities, the Galaxy S23 Ultra was distinguished by its 10x zoom, which was one of its feature highlights. Consequently, the prospective move backward appeared to be perplexing, particularly with regard to the specifications.

Nevertheless, let's go deeper into the specifics of the 5x zoom lens that comes with the Galaxy S24 Ultra. It is more of a lateral move than it is a step in the wrong direction. In point of fact, the Galaxy S24 Ultra is equipped with the most advanced zoom camera that can be found on a smartphone. It is superior to the 10x zoom of the Galaxy S23 Ultra and provides much better performance than the 5x zoom of the best smartphones currently, particularly when it is employed to its full potential.

When compared to its predecessor, the Galaxy S24 Ultra is capable of producing images that have much improved dynamic range and excellent color reproduction when zooming in at 10x or even 100x. The S24 Ultra adds depth and shadow to the photographs, in contrast to the previous model, which had a tendency to produce images that appeared flat. However, in order to improve the overall image quality, certain fine details were sacrificed.

As a result, this compromise is advantageous. The images that were obtained with the S23 Ultra at 10x and 100x zoom frequently looked to be of poor quality, with obvious noise and blur that resembled a virtual salad of digitally sliced pixels. Images captured by the Galaxy S24 Ultra, on the other hand, may not display as much detail as those captured by other devices, but they are significantly more visually appealing thanks to their resemblance to photos rather than forensic evidence.

When the iPhone 15 Pro Max is compared directly to the Galaxy, the iPhone initially performs better than the Galaxy when zoomed in at 5 times. Nevertheless, when digital zoom is used, the Galaxy S24 Ultra starts to perform exceptionally well. At a zoom of five times, both cameras are able to shoot breathtaking landscape photographs of a lighthouse. However, when zoomed in to 25 times, the Galaxy maintains more definition and deeper color. It even allows for distinguishable details such as the stairs that go up from the dock of the Peck Ledge lighthouse, which is located one mile off the coast of Connecticut.

The photographs taken by Samsung have been subjected to criticism in the past for their odd color rendering. This feedback was clearly taken seriously by the corporation, as evidenced by their efforts to bring their processing methods closer in line with those of the iPhone. The end result is colors that appear more natural, and they are typically cooler than the overly warm tones that are prevalent in iPhone photographs. Furthermore, digital sharpening difficulties have been resolved, which has resulted in images captured by the Galaxy S24 Ultra exhibiting a satisfactory level of clarity at the expense of the blurriness that is typically seen in photographs taken with an iPhone.

When all is said and done, the camera does have certain shortcomings. There is still a concern over the low-light performance of the smartphone, as other smartphones are better able to handle situations that occur during the night.

The Galaxy S24 Ultra emerges as the best photography phone of the previous year, taking into consideration all aspects. It is possible that it does not dominate every element, but it routinely beats its competition, whether they are iPhones, Pixels, or even newer OnePlus models that have superior Hasselblad processing.

It is in the ability to take one-of-a-kind photographs that Samsung truly shines. It doesn't matter if you want to take delectable pictures of handmade pizza or gorgeous macro photos up close; the Galaxy S24 Ultra can deliver both. The portraits and selfies that you take are equally remarkable, with skin tones that are realistic and a great deal of detail to ensure that you look your best. Even when it comes to framing topics, such as lovely pets, the phone is able to crop photographs to perfection with ease, offering no difficulty whatsoever.

In terms of photo editing, Samsung has made significant progress; yet, third-party software continues to be the more desirable option. Users are now able to utilize Generative Edit AI tools within the Gallery app of the Galaxy S24 Ultra. These features allow users to resize and rearrange objects, and even make complete backdrop changes based on the context of the image. Despite the fact that it is a cool feature, it is more akin to a mixed-media collage than it is to conventional photography. It is important to note that an artificial intelligence modification will result in the addition of a small watermark to the photograph.

Do not be concerned if you are unable to access the Photo Unblur feature that is available on the Google Pixel 8; Samsung provides a remedy. Navigate to the **Galaxy App Store** and download **Samsung's Galaxy Enhance-X picture editor.** This application offers a wide variety of sophisticated editing capabilities, many of which make use of artificial intelligence and machine learning.

Applications such as Adobe Lightroom and SnapSeed are able to function faultlessly on the Galaxy S24 Ultra, making them suitable for more complex editing tasks. Editing with the S Pen that comes with the device is proved to be more effective than using one's finger.

Samsung claims that its integrated artificial intelligence will be able to distinguish things and identify subjects in order to take good photographs. Whether or not the new model is capable of matching the spectacular astrophotography capabilities of its predecessor, the Galaxy S23 Ultra, is something that needs to be seen.

Performance

Android phones have had a difficult time surpassing the raw performance of Apple's top devices ever since Apple introduced its very own Bionic chipset for the iPhone with its introduction. This, however, is no longer the case as a result of the launch of the Galaxy S24 Ultra. The speed of this powerhouse is not only comparable to that of the best smartphones currently, but it additionally outperforms these smartphones in many respects.

Regardless of the fact that the typical user might not immediately notice these performance increases, credit must be given where credit is due. The silicon produced by Qualcomm and Samsung has, for the first time in years, been able to outperform that of Apple.

What exactly does this imply for use in day-to-day life? In essence, every single activity that you do out on your smartphone can now be completed more quickly. You are able to experience lag-free gameplay at the highest settings, even when playing demanding games like as Call of Duty Mobile or Genshin Impact. This is possible regardless of the game you are playing.

Once you pair your game with an Xbox or Playstation controller using Bluetooth, you will get access to a whole new world of multiplayer gaming. This new world will allow you to easily dominate opponents who are using less powerful devices such as Motorola phones. If you are participating in multiplayer combat, you will have a big advantage thanks to the responsiveness of the Galaxy S24 Ultra to your commands and motions.

But is the Galaxy S24 Ultra a phone that is only designed for gaming? In a word, yes. A head-to-head comparison was conducted between the Asus ROG Phone 8 Pro, a device that was created primarily for gaming, and the S24 Ultra, which excelled it in every respect, even obtaining greater framerates in the most recent titles.

Even if gaming is not your primary use, you will still be able to take advantage of its exceptional performance. In the case of editing photographs in Adobe Lightroom, for example, the Galaxy S24 Ultra enables modifications to be made in real time while maintaining a smooth experience. According to side-by-side tests, the Galaxy S24 Ultra was able to effortlessly identify and pick foreground topics seconds faster than its predecessor, the Galaxy S23 Ultra. This was accomplished by employing Adobe's newly introduced intelligent masking technologies.

The performance of the Galaxy S24 Ultra is, however, hindered by its new artificial intelligence elements, which, paradoxically, result in delays. Notwithstanding the fact that Samsung has been able to outperform Apple in terms of performance, the S24 Ultra was laden with artificial intelligence features that Apple has not yet adopted. Fortuitously, rather than improving the user experience, many additions, such as the ability to compose new text messages or make adjustments in the photo gallery, introduce waiting times.

While these artificial intelligence features hold a great deal of promise, they are not yet worth the wait. The consumers would surely be amazed and use them more regularly if they were as rapid as other services, such as the real-time adjustments that are available in Adobe Lightroom. Every time the AI elements are activated, it feels like it is hitting a roadblock rather than going easily. This is the current state of affairs.

Battery life and charging

It is not necessary to look any farther for a battery life that is superior to what the Galaxy S24 Ultra provides. During our rigorous lab tests, which involve continuous 5G web browsing until the battery empties, the Galaxy S24 Ultra lasted an astounding 16 hours and 45 minutes when it was set to its default Adaptive display mode. Additionally, it outperforms a large number of other Android phones and is superior to the Galaxy S23 Ultra by more than two hours for performance.

If you want to have a longer battery life, you will need to get a high-performance gaming phone such as the Red Magic 9 Pro, which has a significantly larger battery capacity of 6,500mAh.

It is interesting to note that Samsung has not reduced the size of the battery in comparison to the Ultra model from the previous year. Instead, the company has improved the power management on the Galaxy S24 Ultra, which has led to a more efficient utilization of energy. Users are able to simply alter the adaptive screen settings or turn them off to maintain a steady brightness, despite the fact that these settings can be quite severe. Changes can also be made to parameters such as the screen resolution and the performance of the processor in order to reduce power consumption.

There is a "Power Saving" function that Samsung provides, which includes an ultra-power saving mode that is now integrated inside the settings under the heading "Device care." This feature offers even more alternatives for conserving power. This mode gives users the ability to restrict the number of apps they use, disable edge panels, darken the display, and deactivate functions that are not necessary in order to save battery.

On the other hand, among the available choices, there is one that is even more intelligent: "Adaptive power saving." The capability of this feature to evaluate usage patterns and adapt power-saving measures in accordance with those patterns makes it a feature that should be sought out, irrespective of the fact that it is somewhat hidden within the Settings menu.

When it comes to charging, the Galaxy S24 Ultra is capable of supporting 45W charging, which is an impressive speed that increases the phone's capacity to more than fifty percent in just half an hour. As a result of my tests, the phone reached about forty percent in fifteen minutes and completed a full charge in approximately forty-five minutes, which is far faster than the time estimated by Samsung.

In spite of the fact that there are mobile devices that are capable of charging at a quicker rate, such as the OnePlus 12 with its 80W charger, the S24 Ultra continues to be very competitive due to its compatibility with 15W wireless charging, which includes the most recent Qi2 standard. In addition, it provides the capability of wireless power sharing, albeit the capability is slightly concealed within the **Settings menu.** An alternative that would be more convenient would be to incorporate a button for wireless power sharing into the Quick settings menu so that it is easier to access.

Notably, in contrast to the OnePlus 12, the Galaxy S24 Ultra does not include a charger in the box. As a result, consumers are required to purchase a charger separately in order to achieve the highest possible charging speed. You might want to take into consideration the Anker 713 Nano Charger, which is sold on Amazon and has comparable performance at a lesser price point. This is an alternative that is more favorable to your wallet.

Software and support

It is abundantly clear that Samsung is concentrating its efforts exclusively on hardware, while ignoring the enhancements that it is making to its software. The graphical user interface (UI) of the Galaxy S24 Ultra is becoming increasingly difficult to manage, which contributes to the unsatisfactory software experience. Samsung's uncertainty regarding user-centric innovations is shown by the fact that even fundamental functionalities are overshadowed by multiple layers of menus and options.

Even though Galaxy S24 Ultra has a profusion of functions, it can be difficult to locate individual ones. Where are the new artificial intelligence translation tools, as well as the AI service that can rewrite text messages? Where do you activate the artificial intelligence that edits photos or summarizes web pages? The fact that they are all grouped together and hidden under the Settings menu is unfortunate because it makes them unavailable to a large number of people.

This problem is acknowledged by Samsung, which accepts that the functions are concealed within the Settings menu, which is an unusual location for customers to investigate themselves. Attempts to teach users on the capabilities of the phone are hampered by an excessive number of messages and suggestions, including adverts on brand-new handsets, which are not successful in educating customers.

It is necessary for Samsung to optimize its user interface by deleting elements that are redundant and hiding features that are used less frequently in order to stimulate user discovery. Furthermore, the application of AI elements, while excellent in many circumstances, falls short in other instances. The artificial intelligence writing style function, for instance, has a limited amount of usefulness and does not live up to the lavish claims it makes.

Additionally, the Samsung Keyboard has a number of serious problems with its autocorrect feature, which makes typing a very painful experience. The intransigence of the keyboard makes the problem much worse, making it more difficult to repair errors and requiring updated software to be installed immediately.

Although there are certain artificial intelligence capabilities that are innovative, such as generative wallpaper, there are others, such as the Voice Recorder app, that are not even close to being on pace with competitors like the Google Pixel. As a similar point of comparison, the Galaxy S24 Ultra's image editing facilities are not as sophisticated as those found on competing smartphones.

In spite of these software issues, Samsung's DeX functionality stands out as outstanding because it transforms the phone into a desktop replacement that is fully functional. In terms of productivity, this versatility proves to be invaluable, particularly when attempting to balance work and personal responsibilities.

When considering the future, Samsung's pledge to providing software upgrades for seven years poses issues, particularly with regard to the incorporation of developing artificial intelligence technology. Both the possibility of a transition to features that are based on subscriptions and the lack of clarity about long-term support highlight the extent of the uncertainty surrounding Samsung's claims.

When it comes down to it, customers anticipate that Samsung will follow Apple's lead when it comes to software updates, which will guarantee that all eligible devices will have equal access to the features. For the sake of Samsung's reputation and the satisfaction of its customers, it will be of the utmost importance to preserve transparency and consistency in software support as technology continues to evolve.

Release date and price

It is now possible to purchase the Galaxy S24 Ultra, along with its rivals in the series, nearly anyplace that sells electronic goods throughout the world. The Samsung S24 Ultra is available for purchase in the United States from all the major carriers, as well as from retailers such as Best Buy and Amazon. Additionally, it may be purchased straight from Samsung's website.

At the time of its launch, the Samsung Galaxy S24 Ultra fetches a greater price than the Ultra that was released the previous year, which may cause some emotional distress. Although the Galaxy S23 Ultra already had a large number of features, the Galaxy S24 Ultra does not add any ground-breaking breakthroughs; rather, it improves upon the functions that were already present in the Galaxy S23 Ultra.

You should be prepared to pay a significant amount more than the worth of your trade-in if you are thinking of upgrading from the model that was released the previous year. In spite of this, I continue to believe that it is worthwhile to upgrade, at least for the time being. Older phones may gradually lose value with each upgrade that Samsung releases as the company continues to offer new artificial intelligence technologies. This risk is something that should be taken into consideration, particularly in light of the possibility that Samsung will opt to remove functionality from future models like as the Galaxy S22 Ultra or even further.

What about the subject of whether or not the Galaxy S24 Ultra is worth the hefty price tag that it comes with? If you are asking this question, you are probably looking for feedback on the Galaxy S24 Plus, which might provide a better value. By delivering capabilities that are unrivaled by any other device, the Ultra exemplifies the pinnacle of smartphone technology. The normal pricing system is not applicable to it; its value is not based on monetary concerns.

Galaxy S24 Ultra price at the time of launch:

- 256 GB costs $1,299.99
- 512 GB costs $1,419.99
- 1 terabyte costs $1,659.99

CHAPTER TWO

Setting up your device

How to turn on your device and set it up

Note:

- Comes without a physical SIM card and is best activated using an eSIM (embedded SIM card).
- If opting for eSIM activation, ensure a Wi-Fi network is available.
- Offers the flexibility to activate cellular service using either an eSIM or physical SIM.
- Avoid inserting a 4G SIM card to prevent compatibility issues.

Now, let's focus on how to turn on your device and set it up properly;

1. To power on, press and hold the Power button (located on the right edge, below Volume buttons) until the Samsung Galaxy screen appears, then release.
2. Note that Galaxy S24 / Galaxy S24+ / Galaxy S24 Ultra devices do not come with a pre-installed 5G SIM card and are recommended for eSIM activation.
3. Upon startup.
- Select your preferred language and tap the Start icon.
- Review and agree to the 'Terms and Conditions' screen.
- Choose "Set up manually" if not using another device for setup.
- Connect to a Wi-Fi network and input the password. You can skip this step to add Wi-Fi networks later.
4. If activating using eSIM, ensure a Wi-Fi network is accessible.

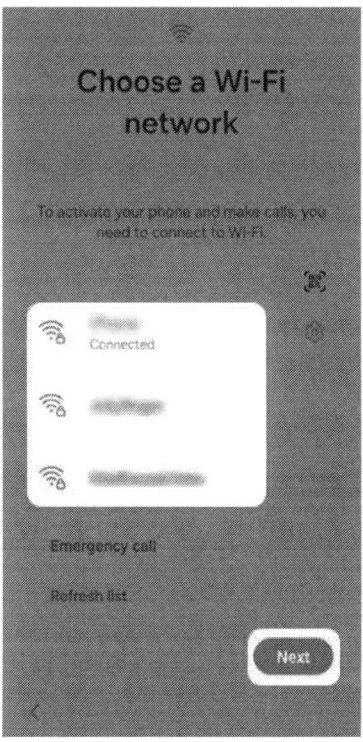

5. If prompted, search for mobile plans and allow a few minutes for activation.
6. You can add an eSIM Profile later in Settings.
7. Complete phone activation by tapping **Next** on the 'Phone Activation' screen and entering the account PIN if prompted. Ensure the old phone is powered off if activating a new phone.

8. Choose your preferred option on the 'Copy apps & data' screen, and refrain from restoring the device during troubleshooting.
9. Sign in or create a Google™ account and agree to the terms.
10. Specify who will be using the device on the 'Who will be using this device?' screen.
11. Agree to the Google Terms of Service and configure Google Services according to preference.
12. Choose a security option on the 'Protect your phone' screen or set it up later.
13. Agree to set up Voice Match and Google Assistant or skip these steps.
14. Enable or disable Verizon Services and accept Verizon Cloud and Digital Secure terms.
15. Sign in or create a Samsung account and agree to the legal information and permissions.

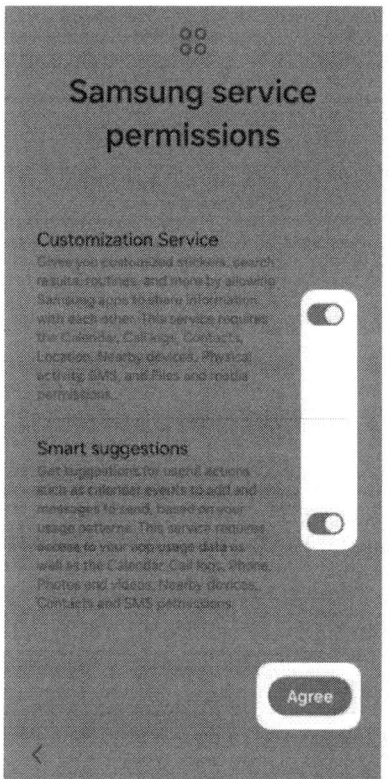

16. Choose your preferred display mode ('Light' or 'Dark') and tap Next.

17. Once the setup wizard is complete, tap **Done** on the final screen.

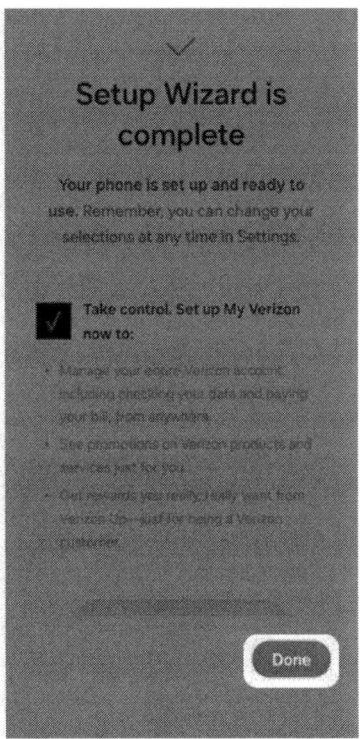

How to set up your device with Fast Pair

Fast Pair is a useful function that can be found on Android handsets. Its purpose is to streamline the process of setting up your new Samsung Galaxy S24 Ultra and other Bluetooth accessories, such as smartwatches and earbud wireless headphones.

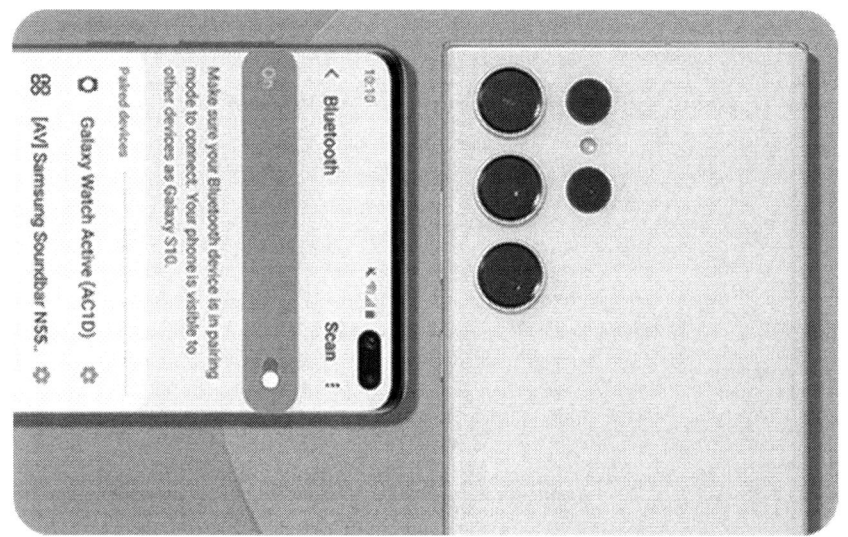

In order to set up your Galaxy S24 Ultra employing Fast Pair, simply follow the steps mentioned below:

- Turn on your brand-new Samsung Galaxy S24 Ultra.
- Your old device should be brought close to the new one, which can be any smartphone that is running Android 10 or a later version.
- On your older device, check to see that both the Wi-Fi and Bluetooth connections are active.
- When you are using your previous smartphone, look for the Fast Pair popup

notice that is titled "Set up Galaxy S24 Ultra," and then hit the "Set up" button.
- Make use of the QR scanner on your previous device in order to scan the QR code that is displayed on the screen of your Galaxy S24 Ultra.
- Pick your preferred wireless network.
- Enter the personal identification number (PIN) of your previous device.
- Tap the "Use QR code to add eSIM" or "Skip" button to determine whether you wish to connect an electronic SIM card.

Easy setup with another device

Sign in automatically and copy settings, accounts, and more from another phone or tablet. Keep your other phone or tablet nearby and unlocked.

Galaxy or Android device

iPhone® or iPad®

Set up manually

- Select "Next" or "Don't copy" to make your decision regarding whether or not to copy the data and applications.
- If you are moving from a device that is not a Galaxy, you will need to download Smart Switch on your previous device and then

follow the instructions that appear on the screen.
- The Smart Switch screen on your Galaxy S24 Ultra should have the "Allow" button tapped.
- You must choose between transferring the data wirelessly or using a cable.
- Your mobile device will look for data that is available to be transferred. After selecting the items you wish to move, select "Next..
- You can accept the privacy page for Google Services by hitting the "Accept" button.
- Choose the search engine that best suits your needs.
- You have the option of either setting up Google Assistant or disregarding this step.
- To proceed, select "Next" from the list of information on the Advanced intelligence screen.
- Accept the permissions that Samsung services require by selecting and hitting the "Agree" button.

- Choose between the light or dark display option that best suits your needs.

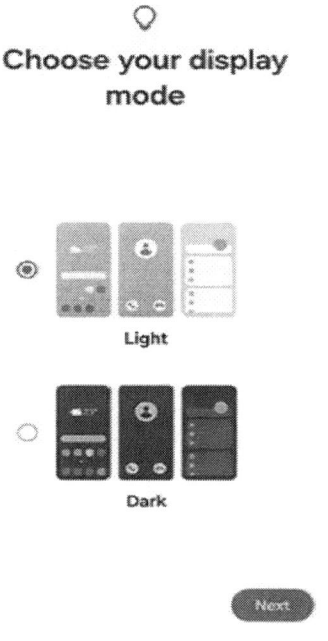

- When you are finished, touch the "Finish" button to finish the setup procedure.

How to insert the SIM card

It would be greatly appreciated if you would abstain from placing the SIM card into the device while it is powered on, as this might potentially cause harm to either the SIM card or the device itself. It is imperative that the gadget be turned off before proceeding in a secure manner.

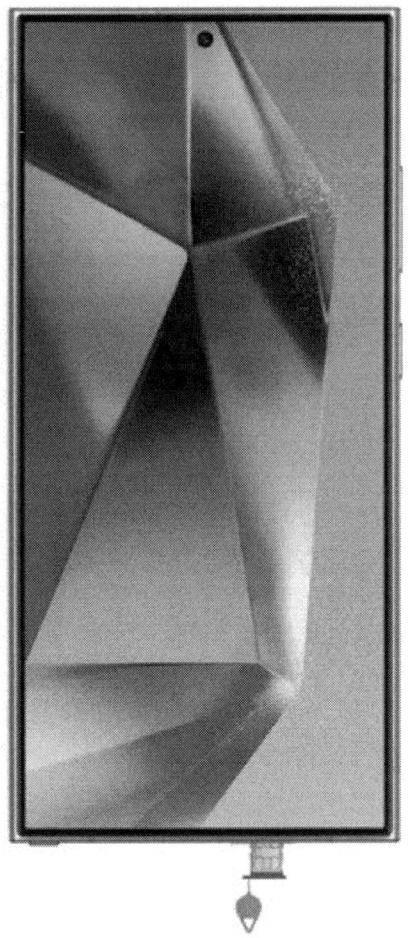

With the display facing upwards, carefully remove the card tray from the bottom edge of the device at the top of the device. The next step is to select one of the following options:

- **To put in a SIM card.**

Ensure that the gold contacts on the SIM card are facing upwards, and then make sure that the card is firmly inserted into the slot that has been allotted for it.

- **To remove a SIM card.**

After removing the tray, carefully remove the SIM card from the tray until it is completely removed. By adhering to these instructions, you will better ensure that the SIM card and device are handled in the appropriate manner.

How to transfer photos to your computer

Using this method, only unencrypted audio and video files can be transferred.

Through the use of the USB cable that was given, you can connect your Galaxy S24, Galaxy S24+, or Galaxy S24 Ultra to a computer by following these steps:

- If prompted to access your data, select "Allow..
- The Notifications panel can be accessed by swiping down from the Status bar located at the top of your screen, if necessary.
- Locate and touch the USB option from the list of notifications. This might be for charging over USB, transferring images via USB, or any other purpose.
- In the event that it is required, press the notification to further expand it, and then select "Transferring files." A dot in blue denotes the presence of this option.
- File Explorer or Windows Explorer should be opened on your device. The Windows key and the letter E can be pressed simultaneously to accomplish this, or you can right-click on the Start button and pick either "Open Windows Explorer" or "File Explorer..
- File Explorer or Windows Explorer should be used to navigate to the "Galaxy S24 Ultra" path. Under the heading "Devices and drives"

in the "This PC" area, you will discover the "Galaxy S24 Ultra". Your particular model (for example, Galaxy S24+ or Galaxy S24 Ultra) or the modified name of the smartphone will be reflected in the device's name.

- You can copy media files by using the computer to move them from the proper folder on the device to the area you want them to be on the hard disk of the computer. You should carefully detach the USB cord from the computer once you have completed the process of transferring files.

CHAPTER THREE

Set up eSIM on your S24 Ultra

Say goodbye to physical SIM cards and hello to a more flexible and easier way to manage your mobile network connections using eSIM technology. This chapter covers both novice and experienced tech enthusiasts exploring the realm of eSIM.

We'll guide you through each stage with helpful hints and unambiguous directions. This section is designed to make sure everything goes well and without any problems, from activating your eSIM to selecting a cell provider. So, seize your Samsung S24 Ultra and let's start this thrilling adventure toward a more simplified mobile environment.

Benefits of using eSIM on your S24 Ultra device

Users of the Samsung S24 Ultra can benefit from a wide variety of advantages thanks to the eSIM technology. Firstly, it eradicates the demand for physical SIM cards, so liberating space within your device and lowering the possibility of misplacing or destroying your SIM card. The ability to switch between mobile carriers without the trouble of physically exchanging SIM cards is made possible by electronic SIM cards (eSIM). This is especially helpful for people who travel frequently or who require various mobile network connections.

Also, electronic SIM cards provide you with increased versatility when it comes to controlling your mobile network connections. Through the use of your mobile device, you are able to simply add or delete mobile plans, eliminating the need for actual SIM cards or visits to physical stores. This provides you with increased control over how you use your mobile device, as well as the ability to transfer plans or carriers whenever it is most convenient for you.

Additionally, in comparison to conventional SIM cards, the reliability and safety of eSIM technology is far higher. Due to the fact that eSIMs are encrypted, it is substantially more difficult for unauthorized individuals to access your mobile network connection. You may rest assured that your data and personal information will be protected to a greater extent thanks to this additional security layer.

Understanding the prerequisites for setting up eSIM

Before we get into the specifics of how to set up an eSIM on your Samsung S24 Ultra, let's first discuss the conditions that are necessary.

Start by checking to see if your smartphone is compatible with the eSIM technology. In spite of the fact that the Samsung S24 Ultra is outfitted with eSIM capabilities, it is recommended to confirm this information in order to be absolutely confident. You can obtain the specifications by consulting the user manual that came with your device or by going to the website of the manufacturer.

The next step is to determine whether or not your cell carrier supports the activation of eSIMs. Before continuing, it is essential to make sure that you are aware of the fact that not all carriers provide eSIM services. You can verify whether or not eSIM activation is available by visiting the website of your carrier or getting in touch with their customer service, respectively.

Step 1: Verify that the device is compatible with the carrier and that it is also supported.

In order to begin the process of setting up an eSIM on your Samsung S24 Ultra, the first thing you need to do is check that your device is compatible with the carrier. It is possible to determine whether or not your device is compatible with eSIM technology by consulting the user manual that came with your device or by going to the website of the manufacturer.

Following the completion of the device compatibility check, the next step is to determine whether or not your mobile carrier enables eSIM activation. In order to inquire about eSIM services, you can visit the website of your carrier or get in touch with their customer support. They will give you the information and instructions you need to activate eSIM on your smartphone with the help of the relevant information.

Step 2: Activate your electronic SIM card with your carrier.

After ensuring that your device is compatible with the carrier and that it supports the carrier, it is now time to activate your eSIM with the carrier of your choice. Although the procedure might be different for you depending on the carrier you use, in general, you will need to complete these steps:

- In order to begin the process of activating your eSIM, you should either contact the customer service team of your carrier or visit their website.
- Also, supply the essential information, which may include the IMEI number of your device as well as any other details that may be requested.
- If you want to finish the process of activating your eSIM, you should follow the instructions that your carrier gives you.

Have in mind that in order to activate your eSIM, certain carriers may require you to go to a store. In situations like these, you should make an appointment and bring your Samsung S24 Ultra along with any identification or papers that may be requested.

Step 3: Installing an eSIM plan on your Samsung S24 Ultra

If you have successfully activated eSIM with your carrier, you may then proceed to add an eSIM plan to your Samsung S24 Ultra by following these steps:

- First and foremost, launch the Settings app on your device.
- After that, proceed to the "Connections" area of the website.
- Choose "SIM manager" or another option that is comparable.
- For the option to add an eSIM, select it.
- If you want to scan the QR code or input the activation code that was provided by your carrier, follow the directions that appear on the screen.
- After the eSIM plan has been uploaded, you may start customizing the settings and preferences to meet your requirements exactly.

Step 4: Make eSIM your primary or secondary SIM card if you want to.

Your Samsung S24 Ultra now has the ability to function as either your primary or secondary SIM card, thanks to the addition of the eSIM plan.

- First and foremost, launch the Settings app on your device
- After that, proceed to the "Connections" area of the website.
- Choose the "SIM card manager" option from the menu.
- To determine which eSIM plan you wish to use as your primary or secondary, select it.
- Turn on the option to make use of the eSIM that you have chosen as the default SIM for making calls, sending messages, and accessing data.

It is important to note that the particular steps may change based on the software version of your device. If you require assistance, simply consult the user manual that came with your S24 Ultra device or get in touch with the manufacturer's support team.

Step 5: In the fifth step, simply address the most common eSIM setup issues.

You might run across certain frequent problems throughout the process of setting up your eSIM, even though it is normally uncomplicated. To help you debug, here are some suggestions:

- During the process of setting up your eSIM, you need to make sure that your device is successfully connected to the internet.
- After restarting your device, you should attempt to set up your eSIM once more.
- It is imperative that you verify that you have entered the right activation code or that you have scanned the QR code accurately.
- If you continue to experience problems, you should get in touch with the customer care department of your carrier for assistance.

It is important to remember to contact your carrier in order to receive individualized support, as each carrier may have different criteria or procedures to take in order to troubleshoot.

Additional tips and recommendations for using the eSIM on your S24 ultra

By this period, I hope you must have successfully set up your Samsung S24 Ultra with an e-SIM card. Well, let's now have a look at some extra suggestions and ideas that will help you get the most out of your eSIM experience:

- **Backup Your eSIM Profiles**: Make sure that you back up your eSIM profiles on a regular basis in order to avoid losing any mobile plans in the event that your device is not returned or is damaged.

- **Investigate a Number of Mobile Carriers and Plans**: Get the most out of the adaptability that eSIM provides by investigating a number of different mobile carriers and plans to locate the one that is the most suitable for your requirements. With eSIM technology, switching between different carriers is now simpler than it has ever been.

- **Maintain a Constant Awareness of Your eSIM Usage:** It is important to maintain awareness of your eSIM usage in order to prevent exceeding data restrictions or incurring additional charges. The majority of gadgets come pre-installed with capabilities that can assist you in successfully monitoring how much data you are using.

- **Become comfortable with the eSIM Management Options:** Make sure you give yourself enough time to become comfortable with the eSIM management options that are accessible on your device. The features that fall under this category include the ability to manage roaming preferences, establish data limitations, and more.

If you follow these advices, you will be able to make the most of the benefits that your eSIM-enabled Samsung S24 Ultra has to offer and have a mobile experience that is completely smooth.

In closing, you may unlock the full potential of your Samsung S24 Ultra and take advantage of the ease and adaptability offered by eSIM technology by following the five simple steps that are detailed in this chapter. These steps include validating the compatibility of your device, confirming that your carrier supports eSIM, activating eSIM, adding an eSIM plan, and setting all of your preferences.

Consequently, make the most of this opportunity, get your hands on a Samsung S24 Ultra, and be ready to embark on this thrilling path toward a mobile experience that is more simplified with eSIM.

CHAPTER FOUR

Message Delivery Report

It is possible that it is vital for you to check the delivery and read status of your text messages if you are using a Samsung Galaxy S24 Ultra. To your good fortune, the device comes equipped with a function that enables you to activate message delivery reports. The following is a straight-forward guide that will enable this feature:

How to turn on Message delivery on your S24 Ultra device

You have the option of activating or turning on the message delivery report feature on the Samsung S24 Ultra in order to verify whether or not your message has been transported successfully. It is important to note that this functionality is only operational when the device belonging to the recipient is both powered on and receiving a signal.

To activate the feature that provides a report on the delivery of messages, follow these steps:

- Turn on your Samsung Galaxy S24 Ultra and launch the Messages application.
- The three dots that are positioned in the upper-right hand corner of the screen should be tapped.
- From the menu that drops down, choose "Settings."
- The "More settings" option can be accessed by navigating to the "Settings" menu and then tapping on it.
- Tap on the "Text messages" section after selecting it from the menu.
- Switch the "Show when delivered" option to the "on" position.

- Let us assume that you have enabled message delivery reports, you will be notified whenever your message is delivered to the device of the recipient.

Keep in mind that this function is only active when the device belonging to the recipient is both powered on and receiving a signal.

How do I know if a text message was received

Assuming that you have enabled message delivery reports, you will be subject to a notification after your message has been delivered to the device of the recipient. It is essential to keep in mind, however, that the receipt of this notification does not in any way imply that the receiver has viewed your message already.

Within the Messages app, you have the ability to activate read receipts, which will allow you to make sure that your message has been read. Also, be advised that in order for read receipts to function, the recipient must also have enabled this feature.

Reasons you are not getting delivery reports

If you are not receiving delivery reports, you may be wondering Why? There could be a number of causes for this:

- In the first place, check to see if the feature has been activated under the settings of the Messages app.
- If you have done so and are still not receiving delivery reports, it is conceivable that the recipient's device is either not powered on or is experiencing a loss of signal.
- You might not be receiving delivery reports because some carriers do not support them, which is another possible explanation for why you are not receiving them.

Reasons why SMS messages not delivered

Well, there are a number of potential reasons that could be the cause of your SMS messages not being delivered if you are experiencing problems with such texts. First things first, check to see that you are connected to the internet and that you have a strong signal reaching your device.

Confirm that the gadget that is being sent to the recipient is powered on and that it is receiving a signal. If you continue to experience problems, you might want to try resetting your device or getting in touch with your carrier for additional support.

How do I know someone ignores my text message

Now, if someone is ignoring your text messages, you will not receive any notifications showing that your messages have been delivered or viewed. This is because they are receiving your messages. On the other hand, it is essential to keep in mind that the reason someone is not replying to your messages could be due to a number of factors, such as the fact that they are busy or that they have not seen the message.

How to find out if your number is blocked

When someone blocks your number on a Samsung Galaxy, you will not be able to send them text messages or make phone calls. This is because your number will be blocked. In addition, you will not be notified in any way that your messages have not been sent to the intended recipient through any means.

When you have reason to believe that someone has blocked your phone number, you should make an effort to get in touch with them or send a message from a different number.

Reasons some text might say 'read' and others don't

To answer the question of why some text messages show the word "read" and others do not, the answer lies in the fact that the Messages app determines whether or not read receipts are enabled. In the event that you have activated this feature, you will be notified when the receiver has finished reading your message. It is important to keep in mind, however, that read receipts are only functional if the recipient has likewise configured this feature.

In situations where the recipient has not enabled read receipts, you will not be notified when they read your message because you will not receive a signal to that effect. It is also possible that the messaging app you are using does not support read receipts, which is another reason why it is possible that the app you are using does not have this capability.

To summarize, activating message delivery reports on your Samsung Galaxy S24 Ultra offers a straightforward approach to verify whether or not your text messages have been sent to the device of the recipient. However, keep in mind that in order to receive delivery reports, the recipient's device must be powered on and have a signal. Restarting your smartphone or contacting your carrier for assistance are two options to explore if you are experiencing problems with sending or receiving text messages.

How to change text notification sound

Making adjustments to the sound that plays when you receive a text notification on your Galaxy S24 Ultra is a straightforward process that can be finished in a few simple steps. You won't have any trouble handling your text messages, regardless of whether you're using the Galaxy S24 Ultra or another Galaxy device.

Through the customization of the notification sound, you will be able to instantly recognize the individuals who have sent you messages. Detailed instructions on how to modify the sound that plays when you receive a text notification on your Galaxy S24 Ultra can be found below.

On top of that, personalizing the sound of the text notification is really advantageous because it guarantees that you will not overlook any significant messages from crucial connections. Whenever you get a text message, you may immediately check your Galaxy S24 Ultra and read the message without any delay.

Modify the sound of the text notification on the Galaxy S24 Ultra.

In addition, you have the ability to program a personalized notification sound to be played whenever particular conversations or text messages are received. By making use of this function, you will be able to determine whether or not a message is originating from a conversation in which you are actively participating.

Guidelines for Altering the Sound of the Text Notification on the Galaxy S24 Ultra

On their Galaxy smartphones, the majority of users most frequently use either Samsung Messages or Google Messages as their primary messaging applications. There is a little difference in the settings between these two applications; therefore, it is necessary to determine which one you are making use of.

- To make Samsung Messages the default, navigate to the applications menu and select the Samsung Folder from the category list.
- You should choose **Samsung Messages** and make it the default messaging app on your device.

Changing the default settings for Google Messages:

- Select the messages icon located on the home screen, and then select the option to "Set default SMS app."

- You should choose Google Messages and make it the default messaging app on your device.

Following the instructions below, you will be able to modify the sound that your Galaxy S24 Ultra makes when it receives a text notification once you have identified which messaging app is your default.

Samsung Messages App

- First and foremost, launch **Samsung Messages app.**
- In the main screen of Messages, tap the icon that looks like more options.
- Choose "Settings," which will bring up a new window for you to select.
- You need to make sure that the "Show notification" switch is turned on.
- Make your selection under "Notification categories," and then click on "New messages..

- To view the available ringtones and choose the one that best suits your preferences, tap the "Sound" button.

Google Messages App

- You can access your Google profile by tapping the icon that represents messages on the home screen.
- Make sure to select "Messages settings," and then select "Notifications."
- Check to see that the "Allow notifications" option is turned on.
- By selecting "Notification categories" and tapping "Incoming messages," you may then select "Sound."
- Personalize the sound to suit your own tastes.
- There is no need for you to manually save your modifications because they will be effectively implemented automatically. There will be an update to the sound of your text notice after it is finished.

In the end, you have the ability to alter the sound that is used for the notice, and you can even use a custom file (for example, an MP3) that you have made or downloaded all by yourself. You need only go to My Files, locate the file you want to copy, and then copy it into the Notifications folder that is located under **Internal Storage.**

Whenever you receive new messages, the notification sound that you have selected will play automatically whenever you receive them. In conclusion, the procedure for modifying the sound of the text notification on your Galaxy S24 Ultra has been completed.

CHAPTER FIVE

Camera Feature

Are you looking to take your photography to the next level? The Samsung S24 Ultra camera is now available for purchase! When it comes to creating amazing photographs and videos, this camera is a game-changer since it is loaded with cutting-edge features and technology that is at the cutting edge of technology. However, where do you even start? It is easy to feel overwhelmed when there is a large number of features and options to choose from. This is the reason why we have compiled this detailed reference to the camera that comes with the Samsung S24 Ultra.

In order to empower you to seamlessly generate content of professional quality, we will lead you through each stage, beginning with understanding the foundations and progressing to delving into the more sophisticated settings. Regardless of whether you are an experienced photographer or just starting out, this chapter is the best companion you could ask for in order to realize the full potential of your abilities. Consequently, take your camera with you, and let's get started on our adventure together!

Understanding the Camera Feature

The Samsung Galaxy S24 Ultra is not an exception to the rules when it comes to the superb photographic skills that have been regularly praised for the Galaxy Ultra line of smartphones. Our ranking of the best camera phones includes this most recent iteration, which appears to be in a position to compete for the top spot.

During Samsung Galaxy Unpacked, the Galaxy S24 Ultra was shown to the public. It is similar to its predecessor, the Galaxy S23 Ultra, in many respects, with the exception of one noteworthy improvement: the telephoto camera. While the telephoto lens with a resolution of 10 megapixels and 10 times optical zoom has been replaced with a camera with a greater resolution of 50 megapixels and 5 times optical zoom, the trade-off is a drop in optical range that is countered by an improvement in detail. Through the use of artificial intelligence-based image processing and cropping, Samsung is able to simulate a 10x magnification, providing customers with improved capabilities without the requirement of a physical 10x lens.

The incorporation of artificial intelligence goes beyond zoom capabilities and encompasses the entire camera suite of the Galaxy S24 range. The photographic setup of the Ultra model comes with the promise of a variety of cutting-edge features. Continue reading to obtain a detailed description of the camera technology that is included in the Samsung Galaxy S24 Ultra.

Specifications of the Samsung Galaxy S24 Ultra Cameras

Before we get any further into the capabilities of the camera on the Samsung Galaxy S24 Ultra, let's take a quick look at its specifications:

- Main Camera: 200MP f/1.7
- Ultra-wide Camera: 12MP f/2.2
- Telephoto Cameras: 50MP f/3.4 periscope lens with 5x optical zoom, 10MP f/2.4 with 3x optical zoom
- Front Camera: 12MP f/2.2

Building upon the foundations that were established by its predecessor, the camera system of the Samsung Galaxy S24 Ultra offers increased flexibility. Samsung has introduced the new ProVisual AI Engine, which enhances the capabilities of the cameras in the S24 series. This is in contrast to the fact that the main, ultra-wide, and 3x telephoto cameras have remained essentially untouched.

In terms of practical application, this means considerable gains in delivering photographs that appear more natural and increased performance in low-light conditions, with the 50-megapixel 5-times telephoto camera being particularly noticeable in this regard. Users can anticipate superior outcomes in zoomed-in images and videos in challenging lighting circumstances as a consequence of the increased image stabilization and 1.6 times bigger pixels.

In addition, Samsung has created an algorithm that guarantees the acquisition of high dynamic range (HDR) photographs in a consistent manner, even while using third-party applications such as Instagram. By doing so, users are able to streamline the process by eliminating the need to move between several camera applications.

"Quad Optical Zoom" is a function that is available on the cameras of the Galaxy S24 Ultra. This capability makes use of high-resolution sensors to do intelligent processing and cropping. This enables optical-quality zooming across a variety of levels, ranging from 2x to 10x, with the assistance of artificial intelligence in pixel processing across different zoom levels and the utilization of super resolution techniques for additional zooming, culminating in the 200x "Space Zoom" capability.

The decision to forego the 10x zoom camera, which operates at a lower quality, ultimately resulted in a camera system that is more adaptable. It might be argued that selecting a 5x optical zoom provides greater practicality without sacrificing the ability to zoom in to a higher extent.

Internal Artificial Intelligence Capabilities for the Samsung Galaxy S24 Ultra Cameras

The photographic experience on the Samsung Galaxy S24 Ultra may be significantly influenced by artificial intelligence, which plays a big role in the process.

With the Samsung Galaxy S24 Ultra, artificial intelligence technology is about to transform the way photography is edited. It intelligently offers tweaks to enhance photographs, such as reducing reflections or completing total image remastering, and it does all of this without requiring advanced editing abilities.

The Generative Edit function, which is similar of the Magic Editor seen on the Google Pixel 8, is one of the most notable features. Making use of the capabilities of artificial intelligence enables a variety of manipulations, such as pixel completeness while cropping or straightening, and it enables users to simply recompose photographs by shifting subjects with a simple tap and highlight. Despite the fact that carrying out this procedure requires a brief period of time, our first experiences suggest that it is beneficial.

Samsung promises customers that metadata identifying AI adjustments will be placed into the photos in order to answer concerns which have been raised regarding the usage of artificial intelligence to manipulate images.

Additionally, this cutting-edge use of generative artificial intelligence extends to the generation of video frames, which makes it possible to insert additional frames at a rate of 120 frames per second. This makes it possible for users to simply convert regular video footage into slow-motion sequences, which is great for fixing mistimed recordings of events such as car races or fireworks displays.

As we await the opportunity to thoroughly evaluate the Galaxy S24 Ultra's camera and photography capabilities, initial impressions suggest that its adaptable camera system and AI-driven features hold significant promise.

Camera settings for capturing Photos

Understanding how to adjust the settings on your Samsung S24 Ultra camera is really necessary if you want to take photographs of great quality. The following is a list of important settings that you ought to be familiar with:

- **HDR (High Dynamic Range)**

HDR, which stands for "High Dynamic Range," is a setting that gives you the ability to capture precise details in sections of your photographs that are either exposed or illuminated. By activating high dynamic range (HDR), the camera will take many images at different exposure levels and then combine them into a single image. This will ensure that the lighting is balanced.

- **Live Focus**

By utilizing Live Focus, you are able to effortlessly blur the background of your photographs, thereby drawing attention to the topic of the photograph. Because of this function, you have the ability to change the blur strength either before or after the image is captured, which allows you to achieve the best possible focus on the subject you want to photograph.

- **Single Take**

With Single Take, you can streamline your photography experience by capturing several photographs and videos with just one press of the shutter button. This function allows you to simplify your photographic experience. With the use of artificial intelligence, the camera will then select the best photos, removing the anxiety associated with missing any priceless moments.

- **Food Mode**

Through the use of Food Mode, you can take your food photography to the next level. This mode is designed to enhance the colors and details of your culinary creations, which ultimately results in more appealing food photographs.

- **Night Mode**

Even in low-light settings, you can take stunning photographs using the Night Mode feature of your camera. This setting delivers exceptional results regardless of the lighting circumstances since it takes many photographs and combines them into a single image. The images produced by this setting are vibrant and clear.

Through the process of becoming familiar with these important settings, you will be able to unleash the full potential of your Samsung S24 Ultra camera and take your photographic talents to new heights.

Advanced camera settings for capturing videos

In order to make videos that are compelling and to unleash the full power of the Samsung S24 Ultra camera, you should become familiar with the following advanced settings:

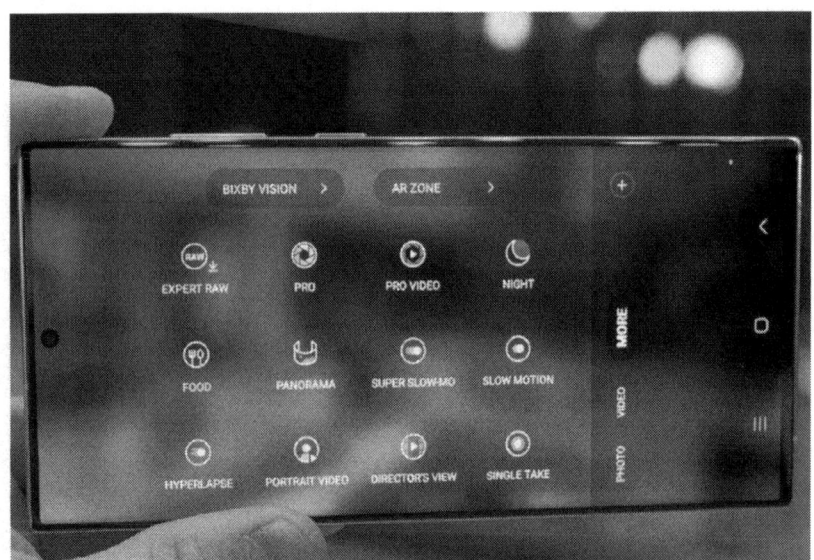

- **Super Steady**

The Super Steady feature makes use of the gyroscope of the phone in order to stabilize your videos. This feature ensures that your videos contain smooth content even while you are moving about.

- **Pro Video Mode**

In Pro Video Mode, you have the ability to manually alter important settings such as shutter speed, ISO, and white balance, allowing you to take control of the video making process. With such a high level of control, you will have the ability to customize your videos to meet your individual requirements.

- **Director's View**

Gain a fresh viewpoint with Director's View, which allows you to flip between all the available camera lenses without any interruptions while you are filming. This function makes it possible to record a single video from a variety of perspectives and angles; it offers up new possibilities.

- **Slow Motion**

You can take your storytelling to the next level by using the Slow Motion setting, which enables you to record at slower rates for a fascinating, theatrical look that gives your movie more depth and drama.

- **Hyperlapse**

Using Hyperlapse, you may investigate the dynamic possibilities of time-lapse videos while you are constantly on the move. You will be able to effortlessly capture captivating timelapses with the help of this function, which is powered by artificial intelligence stabilization technology and offers smooth and stable footage even when the subject is moving.

Tips and tricks for capturing stunning Photos

After you have been comfortable with the settings of the camera, the following are some tricks and tips that can help you improve your photographic skills with your Samsung S24 Ultra camera:

- **Embrace the Rule of Thirds:** A visually appealing composition can be achieved by adhering to the Rule of Thirds, which states that your frame should be divided into thirds both horizontally and vertically, and then your subject should be positioned at this intersection
- **Experiment with Different Perspectives:** Instead of taking photographs at eye level, get away from the typical approach and try

out different positions. You can add a sense of mystery and originality to your photographs by taking them from a horizontal or vertical vantage point

- **Take Advantage of Natural Light**: When you have the opportunity, look for natural light whenever you can, especially during the golden hour, which is the time period that occurs just after sunrise and before sunset. During this time, the light is gentle and warm, which enhances the mood and atmosphere of your photographs

- **Zoom In on Details:** Utilize the Samsung S24 Ultra's ability to capture minute details by zooming in on them and taking advantage of its zooming capabilities. Pay close attention to the more subtle aspects of the subjects you are photographing, whether it be the delicate petals of a flower or the mesmerizing glance of a person's eyes

- **Editing**: If you want to take your images to the next level, you may do so by making use of the editing features that are available on your Samsung S24 Ultra camera. To fine-tune your photographs and bring out their maximum potential, you can adjust factors such as brightness, contrast, and saturation according to your preferences

Tips and tricks for capturing stunning videos

In order to capture amazing videos with your Samsung S24 Ultra camera, you will need to be willing to experiment. In order to get your voyage off to a good start, here are some crucial tips and tricks:

- **Make use of a tripod:** Making use of a tripod helps to stabilize your video, particularly when you are using the Super Steady setting. This results in videos that are smoother and appear more professional.

- **Choose Landscape Mode:** Choosing landscape mode, which is horizontal orientation, allows you to maximize the visual attractiveness of your videos by providing a more expansive perspective that is able to translate well across a variety of screen sizes.
- **Investigate Different Camera Angles**: In a manner analogous to photography, investigating various camera angles can provide a sense of depth and excitement to your videos. When you want to create dynamic and interesting film, you should try out a variety of different vantage points and views.
- **Enhance Audio Quality:** Although the Samsung S24 Ultra camera has outstanding audio capabilities, you might want to think about enhancing sound quality even further by incorporating an additional microphone. With this, clarity is improved, and unnecessary noise is eliminated, which is especially beneficial in areas that are busy.

- **Edit Your Footage:** Take your videos to the next level by utilizing the editing features that are already integrated into your Samsung S24 Ultra camera. In order to refine your video, you can trim, crop, and apply filters. This will transform your raw clips into video that is polished and of professional quality.

How to edit photos and videos on your S24 Ultra

The Samsung S24 Ultra camera comes equipped with a built-in picture and video editor, which enables you to edit your photography and video immediately on your mobile device. Learn about the many different editing tools available, such as:

- Enhance or reduce the brightness of your photo or video by using the brightness control.
- Adjust the contrast finely so that it draws attention to the colors and details.

- By adjusting the saturation level, you may either make the colors more intense or more subdued.
- A wide variety of filters can be used to your visuals in order to impart distinctive styles. This feature allows you to easily trim your films in order to remove any unneeded segments.

How to share photos and videos on Social Media

When you have finished taking and editing your photographs and videos, it is time to show them to the rest of the world at large! The following are some suggestions that will help you efficiently share your information on social media:

- **Determine Which network Is Right For You**: Each social media network has its own set of standards for the size of photos and videos being uploaded. To ensure that your content has the most possible impact, you should be sure to use the suitable platform.

- **Make use of Hashtags**: Hashtags are an essential component in enhancing the discoverability of your content with regard to search engines. Make use of hashtags that are pertinent to your content in order to broaden your audience and increase your reach.
- **Engage with Your Audience:** Encourage interaction with your audience by swiftly replying to their comments and messages. This will help you develop a relationship with your audience. Not only does the development of this interaction help to build your relationship with followers, but it also contributes to the expansion of your following.
- **Maintain Consistency:** Maintaining a consistent publishing schedule is essential to developing a dedicated following and maintaining the interest of your audience. To ensure that your material continues to be visible to your audience and continues to

resonate with them over time, you should establish a consistent posting schedule.

Accessories to enhance your S24 Ultra Camera experience

The following accessories will help you get the most out of your Samsung S24 Ultra camera experience:

- The use of an external microphone can help improve sound quality, particularly in busy areas, resulting in recordings that have more distinct sounds.
- You can achieve professional-looking results by using a tripod to stabilize your camera, which will allow you to take stable photos and smooth video recordings.
- Experiment with a wide range of photography techniques by using wide-angle and macro lenses, which gives you more opportunities for creative expression.

- By keeping a dependable power source close at hand, you can extend the amount of time you can shoot, which is especially helpful while you are on the move.

To summarize, the Samsung S24 Ultra camera possesses remarkable characteristics that allow it to capture photographs and videos that are very amazing. Improving your photography talents can be accomplished by becoming proficient with its settings and experimenting with a variety of ways.

When it comes to engaging with your audience and expanding your following, it is essential to remember the significance of sharing your content on social media. Consider incorporating extras such as an external microphone, tripod, lens kit, or battery pack into your experience in order to make it even more enjoyable. You will be able to generate visually captivating content that will leave an impression that lasts with the help of these tools and strategies.

CHAPTER SIX

Object Eraser on your S24 Ultra

If you have a strong interest in photography and a desire to improve the quality of your photographs by removing distracting aspects, then the **Object Eraser function** is an excellent choice for you. In this chapter, we will explain the benefits of using Object Eraser on the Samsung S24 Ultra, walk you through the process of using it, and show you how easily you can improve the quality of your photographs.

What is Object Eraser Feature

This excellent application, known as the Object Eraser, is meant to remove undesired things from your photographs in a simple and straightforward manner. By simply tapping a few buttons, the Object Eraser is able to quickly remove unwanted elements from your photographs, whether it be an unwelcome bystander in the middle of your beautiful snap or an unsightly background element.

Using sophisticated image processing techniques, the Object Eraser feature on the Samsung Galaxy S24 Ultra performs an in-depth analysis of the picture and removes selected objects in a smooth manner. This cutting-edge feature not only helps you save time and effort, but it also removes the requirement for you to use complicated piece of software for altering photographs. The Object Eraser makes it possible to achieve results of professional grade without leaving the comfort of your smartphone alone!

How to use Object Eraser to remove unwanted objects from images

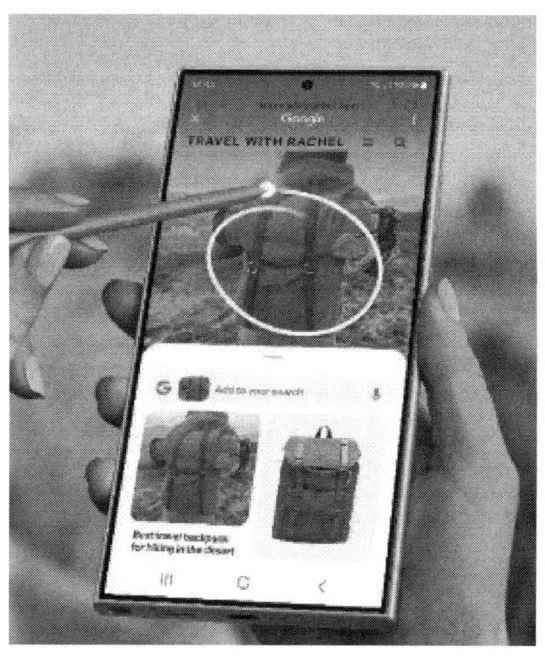

Using the Object Eraser tool on your Galaxy S24 Ultra and editing images is a simple and straightforward process. To get started, you should follow these steps:

- First and foremost, launch the **Gallery app** on your Galaxy S24 Ultra, and then you should select the photo that you want to modify.

- To edit the text, select the Edit icon, which looks like a pencil and is situated at the bottom of the screen.
- Following that, locate the Object Eraser option by tapping on the symbol that represents **More settings.**
- Zoom in on the region of the photograph that contains the unwanted object after picking the Object Eraser option. This will allow for more accurate retouching.
- At this point, you can remove things from the image by tapping on them with either your finger or the S-Pen, if it is possible to do so. The Object Eraser will automatically identify the object and highlight it with a white outline so that it can be removed.
- When you have finished outlining the object, you may then hit the "Erase" button, and you will see the object disappear from your photograph in a miraculous manner.
- If it is necessary, you can modify the edit by altering the size of the brush or by clicking the

"Undo" button to undo any changes that have been made.
- To ensure that the altered image remains in your Gallery after you are satisfied with the outcome, touch the "Save" button.

Benefits of using this feature

The Object Eraser tool that is available on the Samsung Galaxy S24 Ultra offers a multitude of advantages to users who are interested in photography as well as those who are just casual users. Here are some of the most important benefits that come with using this powerful tool:

- **Time and Effort Savings:** You may say goodbye to lengthy photo editing sessions on your PC and save yourself both time and effort because of this. Through the use of the Object Eraser, the procedure is simplified, allowing you to accomplish remarkable achievements in a matter of minutes.

- **Edits of Professional Quality:** The Object Eraser, which is powered by sophisticated algorithms, ensures that your edits blend in smoothly with your photographs, thereby preserving a natural appearance. The intelligent infill method of this program merges eliminated objects in a seamless manner, which results in alterations that appear to have been done by a professional.

- **Professional-Grade Edits:** Simplicity was a primary consideration for Samsung while developing the Object Eraser feature, which is a user-friendly interface. Because of its user-friendly design and basic actions, it is accessible to users of all ability levels, which guarantees a smooth and uncomplicated editing experience.

- **Quality Preservation:** The Object Eraser is exceptional in its ability to remove undesirable things from your photographs while maintaining the quality of the original image. Through the elimination of distractions, it is possible to achieve clarity, color accuracy, and sharpness without compromising.

To summarize, the Object Eraser feature that is available on the Samsung Galaxy S24 Ultra is a game-changer in terms of how smartphone photo editing is done. The ability to remove undesired elements from your photographs and transform them into breathtaking works of art may be accomplished with only a few taps. We bid farewell to those who interfere with your photographs and distract you, and we welcome picture-perfect moments. Get in touch with your creative side and give it a shot right away!

CHAPTER SEVEN

Pairing Earbuds

Is the process of connecting your headphones to your Galaxy S24 Ultra becoming increasingly aggravating for you? There is no need to look any further! Within this all-encompassing chapter, we will lead you through each stage of the process, providing you with clear directions on how to pair your earphones with your device in a seamless manner.

We are here to assist you with anything from configuring the appropriate settings to resolving any potential problems that may arise. However, hold on, there is more! We will also provide you with expert advice to improve the quality of your listening experience and make the most of the capabilities of your earbuds. This chapter is designed specifically for you, whether you are a music enthusiast, a podcast fanatic, or simply someone who wants to completely submerge themselves in the world of audio ecstasy. We will make the procedure of pairing your earbuds with your Galaxy S24 Ultra as easy as possible for you.

How to use the Galaxy Wearable app to pair Earbuds to your new device

These are the steps that you need to take in order to connect your earbuds to a Galaxy S24 Ultra by using the Galaxy Wearable app:

- Make sure that your Galaxy S24 Ultra is both charged and that it is turned on.
- You may find the "Galaxy Wearable" app by opening the Google Play Store on your Galaxy S24 Ultra and searching for it. Download and set up the software.
- Launch the application once it has been installed. Check to see that your earphones are both charged and in the pairing mode. It is possible to enable pairing mode for the

majority of Samsung earbuds by removing them from the charging case on the device.

- A list of the devices that are available to you will be displayed on the home screen of the Galaxy Wearable app.
- In order to begin the process of pairing, you can either tap "Scan" or "Add new device.
- After that, the application will start looking for nearby devices. Tap the earphones that appear on the list to pick them when they are displayed.
- Make sure that the pairing request on your earphones is confirmed by hitting the "OK" button or by following the instructions that appear on the screen.
- At this point, the Galaxy Wearable app will initiate the pairing procedure, which may take a few moments to finish. A message of confirmation will be sent to your Galaxy S24 Ultra once the pairing process has been completed successfully.

- Using the Galaxy Wearable app, you can now modify the settings of your earphones to suit your preferences.
- The equalizer may be adjusted, touch controls can be customized, features such as ambient sound can be enabled or disabled, and more can be done.
- Whenever your Galaxy S24 Ultra is within range of your headphones and Bluetooth is turned on your phone, your earbuds will automatically connect to your phone. This will happen once the initial setup has been completed.

The end of it! It appears that you have successfully associated your headphones with your Galaxy S24 Ultra by making use of the Galaxy Wearable application.

Troubleshooting common pairing issues

It is possible that you will experience difficulties in the process of pairing your headphones with your Galaxy S24 Ultra on occasion, even though you will make every effort to do so. The following is a list of frequent problems, along with potential remedies that can assist you in troubleshooting:

- **Initially, the earbuds are unable to enter the pairing mode.**

If you are unable to get your earbuds to enter pairing mode, you might try having them reset. To accomplish this, you will typically need to press and hold the power button for a predetermined amount of time until the LED light either flashes or illuminates completely. After your earphones have been reset, you should make another effort to insert them into the pairing mode.

- **Galaxy S24 Ultra is unable to detect your earbuds.**

In the event that your Galaxy S24 Ultra is unable to recognize your headphones, check to see that they are in pairing mode and that Bluetooth is turned on. Make an effort to reset your earbuds and put them back into pairing mode if they continue to be unidentified during your search.

- **Earbuds are experiencing intermittent disconnections.**

It is important to check the Bluetooth range between your phone and your earbuds. It is also important to make sure that both devices are within a range of around thirty feet of each other, but this range may change depending on the ambient conditions and the model of your phone. Be careful not to use the devices in close proximity to any impediments that could potentially interfere with the Bluetooth signal. These obstructions include walls, routers, electrical equipment, and electromagnetic interference.

- **Examine the Software for Any Updates.**

Verify that the software on your earphones has been updated to the most recent version. You are able to accomplish this by installing the Galaxy Wearable app on your mobile device and checking for updates.

How to optimize your Earbud experience

Now that you have successfully connected your earphones to your Galaxy S24 Ultra, it is time to improve the quality of your listening experience. The following are some suggestions that will assist you in making the most of your earphones potential:

1. **First and foremost, make use of the equalizer.**

The Galaxy S24 Ultra comes with an equalizer that is built right in, giving you the ability to customize the sound of your earphones to suit your own hearing preferences. By going to Settings > Sounds and Vibration > Advanced Sound Settings > Sound Quality and Effects > Equalizer, you will be able to use the equalizer. The bass, treble, and other sound settings can then be adjusted to suit your preferences from that point on.

2. **Afterwards, turn on the ambient sound feature.**

The Samsung Galaxy Buds Pro and the Jabra Elite 85t are just two examples of earbuds that come equipped with an ambient sound capability. This feature allows you to listen to music while still being aware of your surroundings. It is necessary to locate the "Ambient Sound" or "Transparency Mode" option within the settings of your earbud in order to activate this feature.

3. **Make Sure It Fits Correctly.**

The comfort level and sound quality of your earbuds are both strongly impacted by how well they fit. It is important to make sure that the ear tips you are using for your earbuds are the appropriate size, and you should also try out different positions in your ears to achieve the most comfortable and secure fit possible.

Without further ado, it is a simple operation that can be finished in just a few steps, and it is possible to connect your headphones to your Samsung Galaxy S24 Ultra. After the headphones have been synced, you can personalize your listening experience by making use of the equalization and ambient sound functions that are built in. There is a broad variety of fantastic earbud selections accessible, so it is highly likely that you will be able to locate a pair that is a perfect match for your requirements.

CHAPTER EIGHT

Wi-Fi Calling Feature

Have you had enough of having your calls dropped or having terrible cellphone reception experiences? One should count themselves quite fortunate if they are the proud owners of a Galaxy S24 Ultra. Instead of relying simply on cellular coverage, this cutting-edge smartphone comes with a useful feature known as Wi-Fi Calling, which enables you to make and receive calls by utilizing a Wi-Fi network at the same time. With the help of this chapter, you will be able to activate and make use of Wi-Fi Calling on your Galaxy S24 Ultra, which will ensure that you have uninterrupted connectivity regardless of where you are.

The requirements to use Wi-Fi calling on your S24 ultra

Make sure that you have the following equipment in order to make use of the Wi-Fi Calling feature on your Samsung Galaxy S24 Ultra:

- A postpaid voice and LTE data wireless package that works on a monthly basis. It is not possible for prepaid clients to make use of Wi-Fi Calling.
- An LTE SIM card that has been connected to your device.
- The Wi-Fi Calling option that has been activated on your digital device.

After ensuring that these conditions have been met, check to see if the Wi-Fi Calling feature on your smartphone is activated. You will be able to make calls and send messages via Wi-Fi without any interruptions thanks to this.

How to activate Wi-Fi calling

Wi-Fi Calling is activated when your phone is connected to Wi-Fi and a cellular connection is either absent or weak. This enables calls to be transmitted via Wi-Fi rather than through a cellular connection. If you look in the Notification bar, you will see a symbol that represents Wi-Fi Calling, which indicates that it is available.

There is no complicated process involved in activating Wi-Fi Calling on your Galaxy S24 Ultra. Take the following actions:

- Launch the "Phone" application on your Galaxy S24 Ultra, which can be located either on the home screen or in the app drawer. Launch the application.
- Tap the menu icon that looks like three dots and is located in the upper-right hand corner of the screen.
- Choose the "Settings" option from the menu that drops down.

- You can access the options for "Wi-Fi Calling" by scrolling down and tapping on it.
- Toggle the switch that is located next to "Wi-Fi Calling" in order to activate it. It is possible that you will be required to read and agree to the terms and conditions.
- If you follow the steps mentioned above, your Galaxy S24 Ultra now has the capability to be used for Wi-Fi Calling.

By activating Wi-Fi Calling, you will be able to make and receive calls without any interruptions, even in situations where the cellular connection is either weak or unavailable.

How to use Wi-Fi calling

Making calls over Wi-Fi on your Galaxy S24 Ultra is a straightforward process. The following steps need to be taken in order to make use of this feature:

- Take the necessary steps to ensure that your Galaxy S24 Ultra is linked to a Wi-Fi network. It is necessary to have a reliable internet

connection in order for Wi-Fi calling to function properly.
- To use your device, launch the "Phone" application.
- Just like you would for a conventional call, you can either dial the required phone number or choose a contact from your phonebook through the same process.
- You may notice a little Wi-Fi icon or a label that says "Wi-Fi Call" close to the contact's name or phone number if Wi-Fi calling is enabled and available on your device.
- To begin the call, you must first tap the call button. Establishing the call on your Galaxy S24 Ultra will be accomplished through the use of the Wi-Fi network, which will result in enhanced call quality and coverage.
- The end of it! On your Galaxy S24 Ultra, you are now able to make calls by making use of the Wi-Fi calling feature. Take pleasure in the ease of use and dependability that this

function gives to your experience that involves communication.

Take note that if you are unable to locate the icon that represents Wi-Fi calling on your smartphone, executing a reset will bring it back.

What you should do if you face problems using WI-FI calling on your device

However, there is no need to be concerned if you are experiencing difficulties with Wi-Fi calling on your Samsung S24 Ultra. In order to assist you, the following troubleshooting methods are provided:

- Be sure that your Wi-Fi connection is reliable. The performance of Wi-Fi calling could be hindered by signals that are weak or sporadic.
- Verify that the Wi-Fi calling feature is turned on in the settings of your phone. When you want to activate Wi-Fi Calling, go to "Settings" > "Wi-Fi Calling" and then toggle the switch.
- Bring your Galaxy S24 Ultra back to life. In some cases, a straightforward restart is all that

is required to fix minor bugs or connectivity issues.

- If you need assistance, you should contact the customer care team of your wireless provider. Specifically, they are able to provide troubleshooting instructions or discover any account-related difficulties that are preventing Wi-Fi calling from functioning properly.
- When making calls over Wi-Fi, it is important to keep in mind that different carriers may have somewhat different criteria or settings. Since this is the case, it is recommended that you get in touch with their customer service if you continue to experience problems.

Using a Wi-Fi network to increase call quality and coverage is one of the many benefits that comes with using the Galaxy S24 Ultra's Wi-Fi calling feature, which is a great feature that enhances your calling experience. The activation and use of Wi-Fi calling on your Galaxy S24 Ultra can be accomplished without any difficulty if you follow the methods that have been given above. Despite the fact that cellular service may be inadequate in certain regions, the Wi-Fi calling capability allows users to maintain their connection and still enjoy continuous chats.

CHAPTER NINE

Battery Life

When you own a Samsung Galaxy S24 Ultra, you feel a sense of pride; but, the annoyance of having a battery that drains quickly may also be something you are familiar with. There is no need to be concerned because there are several methods that can extend the life of your battery and guarantee that your phone will remain charged for longer periods of time.

In this chapter, we will discuss the variables that contribute to the rapid depletion of the battery and provide you with efficient strategies to extend the battery life of your Galaxy S24 Ultra in order to make it last longer.

Some factors that can cause battery to run out quickly

Prior to digging into methods that can extend the battery life of your phone, it is essential to have a solid understanding of the elements that can hasten the process of battery depletion. The extreme brightness of the screen is one of the most common causes of this problem. Keeping the brightness level on your phone screen at a high level will greatly speed up the rate at which the battery drains. Because of this, it is recommended that you lower the brightness settings down whenever it is possible to do so.

One further thing that contributes to the rapid depletion of the battery is the simultaneous operation of a number of different applications. The fact that every active app uses up resources from the battery highlights how important it is to swiftly close any apps that are not being utilized. In addition, indulging in activities that need a significant amount of power, such as playing video games or streaming video, will quickly diminish the amount of time your battery can last.

How to extend the battery life on your S24 Ultra device

Let's have a look at some of the ways in which you can increase the battery life of your Galaxy S24 Ultra now that we have a better understanding of some of the elements that contribute to the rapid depletion of its battery.

- **Adjust the Brightness of the Screen:** To begin, you should adjust the brightness of your screen. To reduce the brightness of your phone to a level that is more comfortable while also conserving power, navigate to the settings menu on your device.
- **Close Unused Apps:** It is important to close any applications that are not being utilized in order to avoid undue drain on the battery.

When you want to close them, swipe up from the bottom of the screen, and then swipe either right or left.

- **Enable Power Saving Mode:** Make use of the feature that is incorporated into your Galaxy S24 Ultra, which is the Power Saving mode. Your phone's settings, namely the Battery section, should be accessed in order to enable the Power Saving mode.
- **Wi-Fi should be used instead of cellular data whenever possible.** This will help you lessen your reliance on cellular data, which will in turn help you preserve the life of your battery.
- **Turn Off Location Services:** By turning off location services, you may prevent your battery from being considerably depleted, despite the fact that these services offer tailored benefits. In order to save battery, you should disable location services by going into the settings of your phone and selecting Privacy and Location.

In conclusion, getting the most out of the battery life of your Galaxy S24 Ultra is essential if you want to operate it without interruption. By adjusting the brightness of the screen, closing applications that are not being used, activating the Power Saving mode, giving Wi-Fi priority, and regulating location services, you may lengthen the amount of time that your device's battery runs and improve your experience overall. Using these procedures will allow you to get the most out of the battery that comes with your Galaxy S24 Ultra.

CHAPTER TEN

Multitasking

Enhance your productivity with the Samsung Galaxy S24 Ultra, which gives you the ability to manage multiple projects at the same time in a completely seamless manner. The power of multitasking will be brought to your attention in this all-encompassing chapter, which will take you through a complete walkthrough of the process.

We offer full coverage, which includes the ability to customize your screen layout and the ability to initiate split-screen mode. By following these instructions, you will be able to make the most of the multitasking capabilities of your S24 Ultra. Learn how to separate the display on your Samsung S24 Ultra in a simple and straightforward manner.

Comprehending the Split screen on your device

It is important to have a solid understanding of the concept and functionality of split-screen multitasking on the Samsung S24 Ultra before we go into the specifics of this feature. Through the use of split-screen multitasking, you are able to concurrently watch and interact with two different programs that are displayed on the display of your smartphone. By enabling the simultaneous operation of two applications side by side, this functionality makes it possible to multitask in a seamless manner and to carry out various tasks at the same time.

You might, for instance, be typing an email on one side of the screen while simultaneously having a web browser open on the other side of the screen. While it is necessary to cross-reference information between different applications while still retaining productivity, this capability shows to be extremely useful.

It is vital to become familiar with the many methods that are accessible in order to enable the split-screen mode on the Samsung S24 Ultra. Personal preference and the particular applications that you intend to use both play a role in the activation process but in different ways. Let's conduct a more in-depth investigation into various activation mechanisms in the following part.

Benefits of Split-screen Multitasking

The usage of split-screen multitasking provides a multitude of benefits that have the potential to dramatically enhance both your degree of productivity and your overall user experience. Making use of split-screen mode on your Samsung S24 Ultra comes with a number of important advantages, including the following:

- **Increased productivity:** Split-screen multitasking gives you the ability to carry out numerous tasks at the same time, which helps you save valuable time and save unnecessary effort. Since this eliminates the need to switch between apps on a regular basis, your workflow will be streamlined, resulting in enhanced efficiency.
- **Superior skills for multitasking:** split-screen mode allows you to effortlessly juggle various tasks without requiring you to divert your attention away from the activity at hand. Having the option to have two applications open simultaneously makes it easier to organize and complete tasks, regardless of whether you are working on a project, taking part in a virtual meeting, or simply browsing the web.
- **Streamlined information access:** The ability to simultaneously access information from many applications is made possible via split-screen multitasking, which streamlines the process of

accessing information. You can, for instance, review a document or spreadsheet while you are writing an email. This eliminates the trouble of switching between applications, which in turn increases your overall productivity.

Let's go into the process of activating the split-screen multitasking option on your Samsung S24 Ultra now that you have a greater understanding of the benefits associated with this feature.

How to enable Split-screen on your S24 Ultra device

On the Samsung S24 Ultra, activating split-screen mode is a straightforward process that provides a variety of options that may be customized to suit your preferences and the applications you want to use. The following is a list of the widespread approaches of activating split-screen mode:

- Begin by tapping the symbol that represents the **Recent Apps** on the Home screen.
- Find the application that you wish to use in Multi Window, and then press the icon of that application until a menu displays.
- A Multi Window application can be opened by dragging the icon of the application to the desired area on the screen.
- To watch another application simultaneously in split screen mode, select the respective app.
- To leave Multi Window, move the gray bar to the top or bottom of the screen, depending on which view you want.

Your Samsung S24 Ultra will be able to perform split-screen multitasking more easily if you use these ways. You should try out each option in order to discover which one is your preferred approach. After the split-screen mode has been activated, you will have the ability to further adjust the arrangement of your screen in order to improve your experience of multitasking. This will be discussed in the part that comes after this one.

How to customize Split-screen layouts

For your convenience, the Samsung S24 Ultra provides a variety of options for customizing your split-screen arrangement. This gives you the ability to personalize your experience of multitasking to your specific tastes. The split-screen layout on your device can be customized in a number of different ways, including the following:

- **Adjusting app size:** In split-screen mode, you can quickly resize each app window by dragging the slider that separates them. This allows you to achieve the desired size for each app window. Because of this function, you will be able to devote more screen space to the application that you use the most frequently or that you require to view in more detail.

- **Modifying the order of apps:** The app that is located on the left side of the screen is established as the primary app, while the app that is located on the right side of the screen is designated as the secondary app. On the other hand, you can easily switch the placements of the apps by dragging the title bar of either app to the other side of the screen.
- **Exiting split-screen mode:** When it comes to exiting split-screen mode, you have two different alternatives available to choose from. You have the option of either tapping the middle divider or dragging it to either side of the screen, or you can use the back button to return the primary app to full-screen mode.

The Samsung S24 Ultra provides you with a greater degree of control over your multitasking experience thanks to the customization options that are available to you. For the purpose of determining the configuration that works best for you, you are free to experiment with a variety of various layouts and settings.

Troubleshooting Split-screen issues

It is possible to experience some difficulties or constraints when using split-screen multitasking on the Samsung S24 Ultra, irrespective of the fact that this feature was supposed to be seamlessly operational. Listed below are a few troubleshooting suggestions that can assist in resolving any issues that may arise with split-screen:

- **Compatibility of Applications**: Before you begin using split-screen mode, check to see if the applications you wish to use are compatible with this functionality. There is a possibility that certain applications have limited functionality or provide no support for split-screen multitasking at all.

- **Performance of the Device**: Split-screen multitasking requires a specific amount of performance from the device. If you are utilizing split-screen mode and feel that you are experiencing lag or slow response times, you may want to consider dismissing any superfluous applications or restarting your device in order to free up resources for the system.
- **App-Specific Issues:** Using split-screen mode may cause certain applications to display particular limitations or problems. These issues may be specific to the application. You should look through the app's settings or the support manual to see if there are any known problems or possible solutions.

Consider contacting Samsung's customer care or seeking advice from their online forum if you continue to face chronic troubles or limitations with split-screen multitasking. Both of these options are available to you.

Also, it is possible to substantially improve both your productivity and your overall user experience by becoming proficient in the art of multitasking on your Samsung S24 Ultra. Through the use of split-screen multitasking, you are able to handle many things concurrently, which enables you to improve your organization and the efficiency with which you complete jobs.

Through the activation of split-screen mode, the customization of your screen layout, and the exploration of apps that are compatible with your Samsung S24 Ultra, you can maximize the multitasking possibilities of your device. In order to find the configuration that best suits your requirements, it is important to remember to troubleshoot any problems that may arise and to experiment with a variety of alternative settings and layouts. You will quickly become an expert at

Samsung Galaxy S24 Ultra User's Manual

multitasking on your Samsung S24 Ultra if you put in the necessary amount of effort.

CHAPTER ELEVEN

Developer options

It is possible that you are familiar with Developer Options if you are having an Android device. The hidden menu is tucked away within the settings of your phone, and it provides complex capabilities and adjustments that are often not necessary for the common user.

However, it is useful for developers and those who are knowledgeable about technology. The purpose of this chapter is to explain the capabilities of the Developer Options feature on your Samsung S24 Ultra and to walk you through the process of adding it.

How to turn on developer options on your S24 Ultra device

The following actions need to be taken in order to turn on Developer Options on your Samsung S24 Ultra:

- Put your phone's Settings app into the active state.
- In the bottom right corner, select "About phone.
- Make sure to select "Software Information.
- Look for the "Build number" option and then tap on it seven times in a row repeatedly.
- Following the appearance of a notification, it will be confirmed that "Developer mode has been enabled..
- Once you have turned on Developer Options, you can access it by going back to the main Settings menu and scrolling all the way down to the bottom of the page. There need to be

a listing for "Developer Options" under that heading.

What does developer Mode do

An extensive collection of advanced features and configurations that are not available in the default Settings menu may be found in the Developer Options category. Among the characteristics that are applied the most commonly are:

- **USB Debugging**: The USB Debugging feature makes it easier to connect your phone to a computer, which in turn makes it possible to interact with the software on your phone through the Android Debug Bridge (ADB).
- **OEM Unlocking**: This feature gives you the opportunity to unlock the bootloader on your phone, which is useful for installing custom ROMs or making software modifications to your phone.
- **Mock Locations**: This feature allows you to simulate the location of your phone using

GPS, which is helpful when testing applications that are location-based.

The benefits of turning on Developer Mode

It is not uncommon for the average user to not experience any substantial benefits from activating Developer Options. Nevertheless, it has the potential to be an invaluable resource for developers and other expert users.

When Developer Options are enabled, users are granted access to a variety of sophisticated features and options that are not available in the options menu that is typically used. It is vital to enable Developer Options if you desire access to such functionality within the application.

Additionally, Developer Options have the potential to significantly improve the performance of the device. To give an example, turning on "Force GPU rendering" can improve graphics speed, but turning off "HW overlays" can reduce the amount of strain placed on the GPU of the device, which could potentially lead to an improvement in overall performance.

Troubleshooting issues

Should you experience any difficulty in accessing the Developer Options on your Samsung S24 Ultra, the following steps should be followed:

- Check to see that you have carried out the required actions in the correct manner after. It is necessary to hold down the "Build number" button seven times in a row in order to activate Developer Options.
- In order to gain access to Developer Options, you might be required to enter your personal identification number (PIN) or password if you have established a lock screen.
- In the event that you continue to encounter difficulties in accessing Developer Options, you should try rebooting your phone and again attempting to complete the process.

The risks with enabling developer options

Enabling Developer Options on your Samsung S24 Ultra has the potential to expose you to a number of additional dangers. In spite of the fact that none of the functions contained inside Developer settings will inherently cause damage to your phone, enabling particular settings without sufficient knowledge or caution may result in problems that were not specifically intended.

In addition to making responsible use of these options, it is essential to have a thorough understanding of the potential dangers that are linked with Developer Options. These are some of the dangers that are involved:

- **Performance Issues:** Certain settings inside Developer settings, such as "Force GPU rendering" or "Disable HW overlays," have the potential to have an effect on the performance of your phone if they are utilized in a wrong manner. It is crucial to have a complete understanding of the ramifications of these settings, and you should only make alterations if you have a complete comprehension of those implications.

- **Software Instability:** When certain features in the Developer features menu are enabled, there is a possibility that the software will behave in an unexpected manner or become unstable completely. The activation of "Stay awake" or the adjustment of "Background process limit" is two examples of such actions that can alter the working of your phone and may cause applications to malfunction or crash.
- **Security Concerns:** Despite the fact that enabling Developer settings does not in and of itself provide any inherent security risks, there are certain settings that, if exploited, might possibly expose your device to vulnerabilities. When your device is connected to a computer that you do not trust, for example, enabling "USB debugging"

could allow someone to get illegal access to your device.

For the purpose of mitigating these hazards, it is of the utmost importance to exercise caution when making use of Developer Options. When you are working on a specific project, such as app development or debugging, you should only enable the options that you fully understand and actually need. In the event that you are unsure about a particular option, it is recommended that you leave it disabled.

It is important to keep in mind that Developer Options are primarily intended for developers and experienced users who have a comprehensive awareness of the consequences surrounding these options. It is generally recommended that you keep Developer choices off in order to protect the stability and security of your device. This is especially necessary if you are not well-versed in these choices or the potential consequences they may have.

It is possible to get the conclusion that Developer Options is a powerful tool that can be advantageous for both sophisticated users and experienced developers. In order to gain access to more advanced features or settings on your Samsung S24 Ultra, you will need to activate the Developer Options function. It is important to keep in mind that utilizing Developer Options can have an impact on the performance of your phone, thus it is important to exercise caution when doing so.

CHAPTER TWELVE

Creating GIF on your S24 Ultra

Have you ever desired that you could add some uniqueness to your conversations with your loved ones and friends by sending them a GIF that perfectly captures your feelings? If you have a Samsung Galaxy S24 Ultra, you are in for a real treat because it is quite simple to create GIFs on your device. In this chapter, I will demonstrate three straightforward approaches to the creation of GIFs on your Samsung Galaxy S24 Ultra.

How to create GIF from Photos in Gallery

You want to create engaging GIFs with your Samsung Galaxy S24 Ultra? There is no need to look any further! Our in-depth guide will coach you through the straightforward steps necessary to create animated masterpieces directly on your smartphone.

This guide is designed to accommodate both novices and experienced users equally. You'll be able to get the most of the camera app on your Galaxy S24 Ultra by following the straightforward instructions and listening to the advice of professionals.

Creating a GIF from the photos in your gallery is one approach that may be utilized. This method is ideal for stringing together a series of images. In this manner:

- When you want to select numerous photographs, open the Gallery app and continue to press and hold on an image.
- Select the icon that says "Create.
- Choose the GIF format.
- Examine and make changes to the GIF image that was made. Tap the Save button once you are satisfied.

With the steps mentioned above, you should have successfully created a GIF that is now ready to be distributed to relatives and friends.

How to take Burst shot and create GIF with this feature

The following is an updated version:

Also, the following steps need to be taken in order to produce a GIF on your Samsung Galaxy S24 Ultra by using a burst shot:

- After opening the Camera app, check to see that the PHOTO mode is set correctly.
- When you swipe down on the shutter button, you will activate the burst shot mode. After you have finished taking the sequence of photographs, you should let go of the button.

For the purpose of converting the burst shot into a GIF:

- The first step is to launch the Gallery app and choose the burst shot that you want to convert into a GIF.
- Select the icon that says "Create."
- From the available options, select GIF.
- Examine the GIF and make any necessary changes to it. Tap the Save button once you are satisfied.

How to use the Camera app to create GIF

This is the third and final way, which involves producing a GIF directly using the Camera app. This method is perfect for capturing a moment and rapidly transforming it into a GIF. It can be done as follows:

- First and foremost, tap the **Settings icon** that is situated in the upper left corner of the Camera app after you have opened the app.

- Within the Camera settings menu, select the option that says "Swipe Shutter button to create GIF using camera."
- In the Camera settings menu, select "Create GIF," and then exit the menu permanently.
- Simply swipe down on the Shutter button when you are ready to produce the GIF, and then let go of it when you are ready for the GIF to come to an end.
- There will be a copy of your GIF saved in your gallery.

The creation of GIFs on your Samsung Galaxy S24 Ultra is made simple by the three uncomplicated approaches that are presented here. Whether you are putting together a collection of photographs from your gallery or attempting to seize a fleeting moment, these ways of doing things are guaranteed to be helpful. Why then should we wait? Commence the process of making those GIFs, and then distribute them to your loved ones and friends.

CHAPTER THIRTEEN

Outlook Email

Should you be in possession of a Samsung Galaxy S24 Ultra and find yourself in need of accessing your Outlook email, you will discover that the process is fairly simple. The purpose of this specific chapter is to offer you with an overview of what Outlook email includes, as well as a step-by-step instruction for manually configuring your Samsung Galaxy S24 Ultra. Additionally, we will emphasize the benefits of using Outlook on your mobile device.

What is an Outlook Email

Outlook, which was built by Microsoft, is widely recognized as one of the most prominent email services that are utilized by individuals, corporations, and organizations with equal enthusiasm. Users of Outlook have access to a variety of functions, including the ability to send and receive emails without any complications, effectively manage their calendars, and organize their contacts.

Additionally, Outlook provides users with a mobile application that is both comfortable and easy to use, allowing them to access their email quickly and easily when they are on the road.

How to set up this feature on your S24 Ultra

We ask that you take these simple steps in order to manually set up your Outlook email on your Samsung Galaxy S24 Ultra device:

- First and foremost, simply swipe up from the Home screen to open the menu if you are on the Home screen.
- Navigate to the Microsoft folder, press it, and then select Outlook from the menu.
- When you are presented with the option, choose "Allow" if you are prompted to do so.

If you do not see this question, you should move on to the next available step.
- Make sure to select "ADD ACCOUNT," then input your email address before selecting "CONTINUE..
- When prompted, enter the password for your email account, and then "Sign in..
- When you are given an additional prompt, choose the option that says "MAYBE LATER." In that case, proceed to the subsequent step.
- It is now possible to make use of your email account because it has been configured. Go back to the Home screen once again.

Using your Samsung Galaxy S24 Ultra device, you are now able to send and receive emails from your Outlook account.

Benefits of using Outlook

The following is a list of advantages that come with using Outlook on your Samsung Galaxy S24 ultra device:

- **Get access to your email when you're on the move:** It is possible to access your email from any location and at any time if you have Outlook installed on your mobile device. This ensures that you will never miss any critical messages while you are away from your workstation.
- Manage your calendar efficiently: Outlook gives you the ability to build and manage your calendar in a smooth manner, which not only assists you in remaining organized but also guarantees that you are constantly on top of your schedule, regardless of whether it is for work meetings or personal events.
- **Maintain a connection with your contacts:** Outlook makes it easy to store and manage your contacts, which simplifies communication and ensures that you maintain a connection with your family, friends, and coworkers without any fuss.

- **Enhanced security features:** Outl.
- Ook has powerful security features, such as encryption and two-factor authentication, to protect your email and sensitive data. These features provide you peace of mind regarding the privacy and security of your information. Outlook also provides you with the ability to protect your data.
- **Integration with other applications:** Outlook integrates without any problems with other Microsoft applications, such as OneDrive and SharePoint. This makes it easier for team members or peers to work together and share files, which in turn boosts productivity and workflow efficiency.

To summarize, integrating an Outlook email account into your Samsung Galaxy S24 Ultra is a straightforward operation that confers a multitude of advantages at your disposal. You are able to successfully manage your email, calendar, contacts, and other information with the tools that are available to you in Outlook. This allows you to remain organized, connected, and productive even when you are constantly on the move.

CHAPTER FOURTEEN

Tips and tricks on using your S24 Ultra device

Regardless of whether you have lately purchased a Samsung Galaxy S24 Ultra or have been using it for some time, there is a good possibility that you have either removed the plastic wrap or used a protective cover for the device. Even though that ensuring that your new device functions at peak performance is of the utmost importance, it is possible that you have set it up using Fast Pair in order to make a smooth transition from your previous Samsung phone.

Obviously, one of the most important things to focus on is making the most of this high-end technology. In order to be of assistance to you in this attempt, we have compiled a list of the most useful hints, techniques, and hidden features that are available for the Samsung Galaxy S24 Ultra device.

The Galaxy S24, the Galaxy S24 Plus, and the Galaxy S24 Ultra are all versions of the Galaxy S24 that are compatible with these proposals. All the models have been included in our coverage, despite the fact that the S24 Ultra may have some features that are special to it.

Twenty-One Best Tips and tricks for your S24 Ultra device

1. Enhance Your Screen Clarity (S24 Plus & Ultra)

Unlike the Galaxy S23 series, which only had a QHD+ screen on the Ultra model, Samsung has equipped both the Galaxy S24 Plus and the Galaxy S24 Ultra with displays that are capable of displaying in QHD+. These cutting-edge display panels have a refresh rate of 120Hz and a peak brightness of 2600 nits, making them exceptional in terms of brightness.

You will, however, be need to manually alter the display settings in order to experience the highest possible level of image clarity. This is because the QHD+ resolution is not made available by default. Unless you are upgrading from an S23 Ultra that has QHD+ settings, in which case the settings might be carried over automatically throughout the process of upgrading.

The following is a guide that will help you find the optimal display settings for your Galaxy S24 series phone:

- Go to the **Settings menu** and select **Display.**

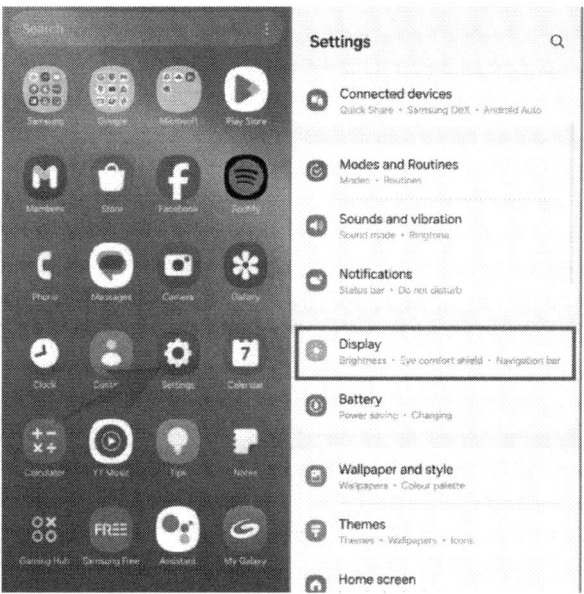

- Select the **Screen Resolution option.**
- Click the **Apply button** after selecting the QHD+ 3120 x 1440 option.

It is possible that selecting a higher resolution will result in a slight increase in power consumption; however, the powerful batteries found in the S24 Plus and Ultra (4900mAh and 5000mAh, respectively) are able to easily manage this situation.

If maximizing battery life is a priority for you, you might want to consider adjusting the resolution to Full HD+ or using Bixby Routines to intelligently transition between QHD+ and Full HD+ based on parameters such as the time of day, the amount of battery life remaining, particular applications, or your location.

2. Create Your Own Unique Generative AI Wallpaper with the Samsung Galaxy S24 Ultra

Discover the full potential of your Samsung Galaxy S24 Ultra by creating unique generative artificial intelligence wallpapers. These wallpapers have the ability to take the aesthetics of your device to extraordinary new heights. With this cutting-edge feature, you may embrace the future of customization, which not only provides visual clarity but also a touch of peace through fascinating animations.

There is a seamless marriage of technology and artistry that is introduced by the Samsung Galaxy

S24 Ultra. This allows you to explore the world of generative artificial intelligence in order to create wallpapers that are suited to your preferences. While the process does incorporate algorithms that are hosted in the cloud, your creative input will continue to be of the utmost importance in molding the final output.

It is possible to bring your vision to life by following this step-by-step guide:

- Proceed to the **Settings app** on your Galaxy S24 Ultra by navigating to it.
- You may access **the Wallpapers and Style section** by pinching on the home screen or by going through the **Settings menu** on your device.

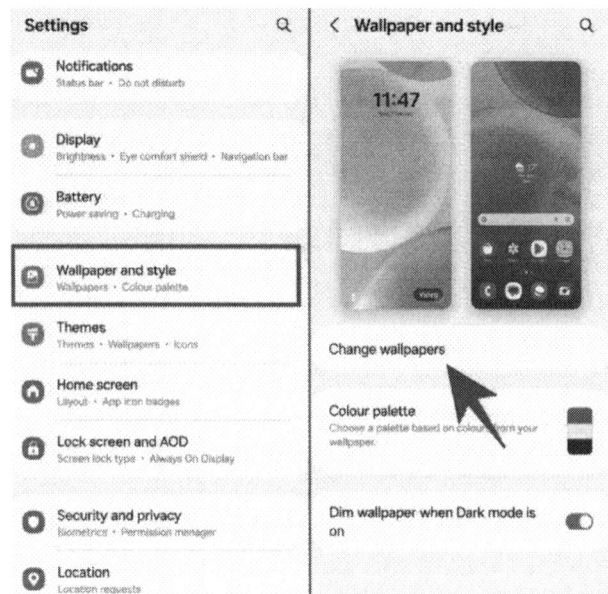

- To get started on your creative adventure, you should look through the **Creative category** and choose the **Generative option.**
- Take a look at the many different themes that are available, and pick the one that best fits your personality and the way you feel.
- Choose highlighted terms that correspond with your aesthetic choices in order to delve deeper into the customization process.
- When you have finished making your selections, you can then press the **Generate button** to watch the magic happen.

Marvel at the magnificent wallpaper that is appearing on your screen; it is a demonstration of the capabilities of generative artificial intelligence as well as the unique choices you have made. You may add a personalized touch to your Galaxy S24 Ultra experience by decorating your home screen, lock screen, or both with this visual masterpiece while you are using your device.

Let's say that your creative instincts seek additional research, you need not be concerned. In order to reveal a new version of your wallpaper, you just only tap **the Generate button** once more. Despite the fact that there is no option to preserve designs that have been made in the past, the virtually limitless source of creativity guarantees that each tap will produce a fresh and captivating outcome.

The bounds of customization are expanded with the Samsung Galaxy S24 Ultra, which provides you with the ability to create a digital atmosphere that is reflective of your personality and interests. Step into a world where creativity and technology coexist, and let your imagination to grow with each stroke of generative AI genius that touches your experience.

3. Enhance Your Lock Screen with Dynamic Weather Effects

With One UI 6.1, we are pleased to introduce the Photo Ambient Wallpaper feature that is available on the Galaxy S24 Ultra. This cutting-edge wallpaper type makes a dynamic adjustment to the background of your lock screen dependent on the time of day as well as the weather conditions that are currently in effect in your present location.

Imagine the sight of fine snowflakes falling down your screen on a snowy day, or raindrops falling across your background on a rainy afternoon. Both of these natural phenomena are possible. Even when the sun is shining brightly, you may still feel the warmth of sunlight coming through your lock screen. Additionally, it offers a stimulating visual experience at any time of the day or night, as it switches between daytime, evening, and overnight without any noticeable transitions.

To activate the Photo Ambient Wallpaper function, you must first navigate to the **Labs section** of the **Settings menu,** then select **Advanced features.** Find the option that says "Photo Ambient Wallpaper" and turn it on by using the toggle switch.

After the feature has been activated, proceed with these simple steps:

- Choose **Wallpapers & Style > Change Wallpapers** from the menu that appears when you open Settings on your Galaxy S24 Ultra.
- Click the **Try On button** after selecting the **Photo Ambient option** from the Creative section of the menu.
- Select an appropriate photograph to use as the background for your ambient wallpaper. If you want the best possible results, choose

photographs taken outside during the daytime hours.
- Pressing the **Play button**, which is located at the bottom-left corner of the screen, will allow you to get a preview of the weather effects.
- Press the **Done button** located in the upper right corner of the screen to save your selection.

At this moment, the intriguing **Photo Ambient Wallpaper** is displayed on your door lock screen. It is important to keep in mind that this function is designed to be experimental; therefore, it may not always accurately reflect the time of day. However, it does provide a fascinating variety of weather effects that can enhance the aesthetics of your device.

4. **Display Lock Screen Wallpaper on Always-On Display (AOD)**

The Always-On Display (AOD) function is a new addition to the Samsung Galaxy S24 Ultra. This feature is a reflection of the Always On feature seen on the iPhone 14 Pro released by Apple. This feature displays important information even when the device is locked. In order to make the AOD display a reduced version of your lock screen wallpaper, the following steps need to be taken:

- You can access the Lock Screen and AOD settings on your Galaxy S24 Ultra by going to the Settings menu.
- Select the **Always On Display option.**
- The option that is called "Show Lock Screen Wallpaper" should be enabled.
- If you have wallpapers that show humans or animals, you might want to think about activating the Erase Background component. Through the use of this function, the primary topic of the photograph is separated from the remainder of the screen, which remains dark.

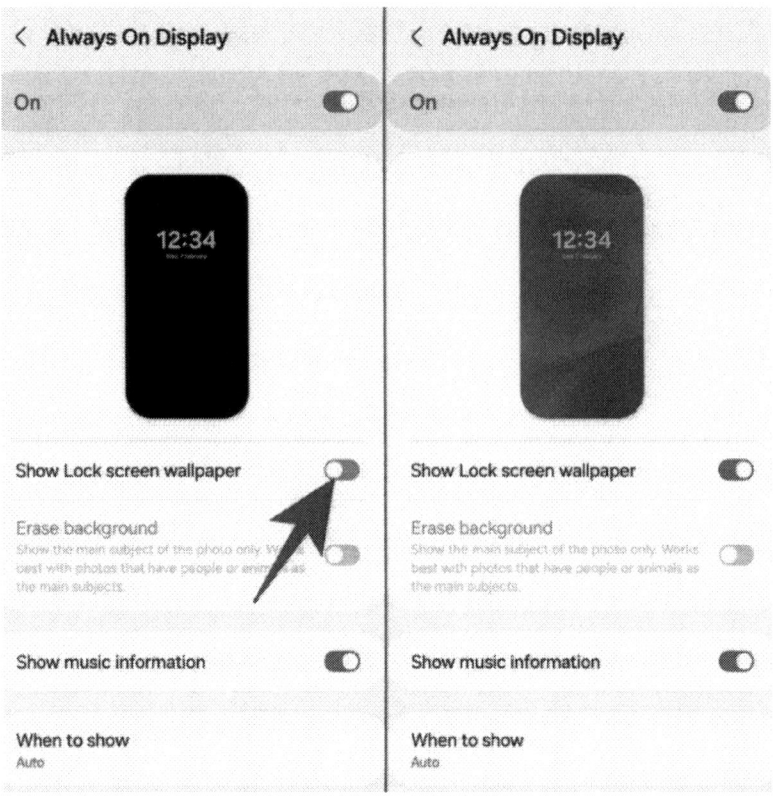

This feature has been fine-tuned by Samsung, which has reduced the screen refresh rate on the AOD and automatically dimmed the wallpaper when the ambient light is low. The ability to erase the background also helps to reduce the amount of power that is consumed.

It is necessary to keep in mind, however, that the usage of this feature may result in an increase in the amount of energy consumption when compared to the usual AOD settings. During our tests with the Galaxy S24 Ultra, we found that the AOD wallpaper consumed around twenty percent of the battery over the course of a day of screen-off standby in a variety of lighting conditions. The brightness of the wallpaper adjusted itself according to the amount of ambient light.

5. Adjust the Phone's UI Colors to Match the Wallpaper

There is a high probability that the elements of the interface (icons, menus, and buttons) on the Galaxy S24 Ultra will not automatically harmonize with the wallpaper you have selected. If, on the other hand, you value the ability to customize the appearance, you can align them. An explanation of how to synchronize the theme colors of the phone with the wallpaper is as follows:

- Take a look at the Settings menu and choose **Wallpaper and Style.**
- Choose a **color palette** instead.

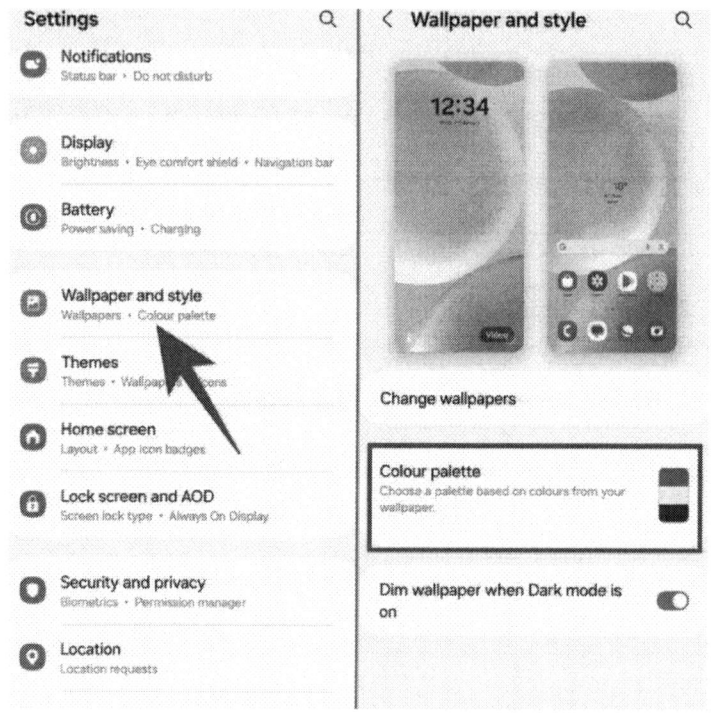

- To select color selections that are derived from your wallpaper, activate the **Color Palette** on your computer. As an alternative, if the color selection does not satisfy your

preferences, you can select one of the basic color options.
- You have the option to enable the Apply palette to app icons feature, which is similar to the themed icons feature that was introduced with Android 12.
- To confirm, tap the **Apply button.**

After that, the color palette will be included into the user interface of your phone, which will include buttons, app icons, the quick settings panel, the lock screen clock, and other components.

6. Activate Light Performance Mode

There are three different Galaxy S24 models: the S24 Ultra, the S24 Plus, and the S24 Ultra. The S24 Ultra is equipped with the most recent Snapdragon 8 Gen 3, while the S24 and S24 Plus, which are more affordable, are equipped with the capable Exynos 2400 chipset that is manufactured in-house.

Sometimes the top-tier hardware muscle is not required for actions that are performed on a daily basis, such as sending messages, browsing the web, or playing back videos. Taking this into consideration, Samsung provides you with the ability to modify the performance of your Galaxy S24 series phone. It is possible to select either the Light mode or the Standard mode, with the Standard mode being the default setting.

By dynamically altering the performance of the CPU in response to the needs of the situation, switching to Light mode extends the battery life of the S24 Ultra and keeps it from overheating. You may activate the Light performance mode on your Galaxy S24 Ultra by following these steps:

- First and foremost, launch the settings menu on your Samsung Galaxy S24 Ultra.
- Scroll down until you reach **Device Care**, then tap on it and choose **Performance Profile**.
- Change the setting from **Standard to Light.**

During gameplay, the light mode will automatically deactivate, allowing for greater battery efficiency during ordinary phone use without impacting the performance of the gaming experience. On the other hand, the Game Booster options allow you to manually customize the level of optimization it provides.

7. Enhance Your Galaxy S24 Lock Screen with Widgets

With One UI 6.1 for the Samsung Galaxy S24 Ultra, you now have the ability to incorporate new lock screen widgets, which are evocative of those found in iOS 16. These widgets make it possible for you to monitor the battery levels of your phone and wearables in a convenient manner, read upcoming reminders, stay up to speed on weather predictions, track Samsung Health statistics, and engage in a variety of other activities straight from the lock screen of your phone.

In order to add widgets to the lock screen of your Galaxy S24 Ultra, follow these steps:

- To begin, click **Settings** and then navigate to the Lock Screen and AOD areas of the menu.
- If you go down until you reach the "Looking for Something Else" section, you will see the option **to Edit** the Lock Screen.
- You will be taken to the editing mode for the lock screen immediately. To add widgets to your lock screen, tap the **Widgets box** that is located below the clock and choose the widgets that you want to feature. Battery, Calendar, Reminders, Clock, Weather, and Samsung Health are some of the widgets that are now available to users.
- Tap the **Done button,** which is situated in the upper right corner of the screen, once you have finished making your selections.

As is the case with iPhones, the Galaxy S24 Ultra feature lock screen widgets that are available in two sizes: 2×1 and 1×1. To cater to your tastes, you have the option to select either two 2×1 widgets, four 1×1 widgets, or a combination of two 1×1 widgets and one 2×1 widget. Any of these options is available to you.

8. Enhance Audio with Dolby Atmos on Samsung Galaxy S24 Ultra

In keeping with the precedent that was established by its predecessors since the Galaxy S10, the S24 series provides support for Dolby Atmos, which provides an immersive audio experience regardless of whether you are listening to the device through headphones or through the speakers. With the help of Dolby Atmos technology, the voices and conversations that are broadcast in video streams are rendered clear and prominent.

Dolby Atmos will take your listening experience to a whole new level, regardless of whether you are listening to catchy pop hits or booming hip-hop beats to music. To get started, this is how to do it:

- To access the Sounds and Vibration settings, navigate to the **Settings menu.**
- Select the **Sound quality and effects option.**

- Make sure that the toggles for Dolby Atmos and Dolby Atmos for Gaming are both turned on.

Despite the fact that the default setting is Auto, you can select from the following presets by tapping on the Dolby Atmos option:

- **Auto:** In this mode, the audio stream is analyzed in order to optimize the sound quality based on the content that is being played.
- **Movie:** A dramatic, three-dimensional audio experience that is suitable for movies, shows, and videos, Movie enhances dialogues, background ambiance, and sound effects to create a cinematic atmosphere.
- **Music:** The music is centered on providing music in the manner that the artists intended, with an emphasis on vocal and instrumental separation for a sound that is more dynamic and deeper.

- **Voice:** Voice is a feature that prioritizes speech clarity, making voices clear and easy to understand. This feature is ideal for podcasts, audiobooks, news, and video conversations.

In addition to Dolby Atmos, you should investigate the following other alternative methods of audio enhancement:

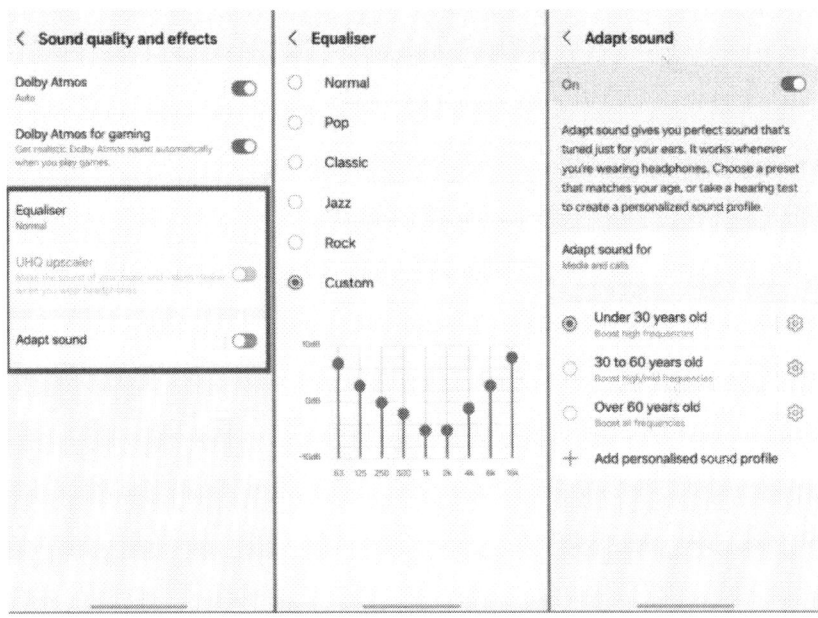

- **Equalizer:** You can use a variety of predefined equalizer settings, such as Bass Booster, Rock,

Classical, and Jazz, or you can manually modify sliders to fine-tune the frequencies of the music. The sound of your music, movies, and other media may be precisely controlled with the help of this additional feature.

- **Adapt sound:** Adapt Sound is a feature that allows you to personalize the audio output for your ears when you are using wired or wireless headphones. It does this by generating a unique sound profile based on how you react to a range of beeps. Whether you use it for calls, media, or both, you can select from a variety of age-based presets to get individualized sound optimization.
- **UHQ Upscaler:** It is a program that automatically improves the audio quality of compressed audio files such as MP3s or streaming music by attempting to restore elements that have been lost throughout the process. When you use wired headphones, this feature will activate, which will improve the quality of your listening experience.

With the help of Dolby Atmos and these extra audio innovations, you can customize the audio on your Galaxy S24 Ultra to align with your tastes for each and every listening situation.

9. Configure Individual Audio Outputs for Each Application

The Separate App Sound feature, which is also available on the Galaxy S24 series, is a brand-new piece of functionality that Samsung has introduced. This function gives users the ability to route audio from certain applications to a variety of outputs, including headphones, speakers, and Bluetooth devices, among other options.

Consider the following scenario: you are traveling with a friend, and you are using Google Maps to navigate while listening to music on Spotify. You would not want the navigation suggestions to interfere with your experience of listening to music. Separate App Sound allows you to assign Google Maps to the speaker on your phone so that you can receive clear directions, and it also allows you to configure Spotify so that it may stream music continuously through the Bluetooth speaker in your vehicle.

Using the Separate App Sound option on your Galaxy S24 Ultra can be accomplished in the following procedure:

- First and foremost, access the settings menu on your Galaxy S24 Ultra device.
- Choose the option to **Separate app sound** after you have navigated to **Sounds and Vibrations.**
- To activate the function, use the toggle switch labeled "Turn on now." You will be presented with a dialog that will enable you to select the application and the audio device. Tap the **Select button.**
- When you want to configure a different audio output for a certain app, select the app your choice. In the event that the application is not

already included, you can add it by selecting "Add apps."

- Go back to the previous screen and choose the audio device that you would want to use for the apps that are designated for use with that device (for example, the speaker on your phone or a Bluetooth audio device).

When certain applications are selected, sound will be directed through the audio device that has been defined, while other applications will use the default audio output, which are often the speakers on the device. Note that Separate App Sound is only functional in situations where the audio output that is selected is different from the primary audio output of the phone. This is a critical point to keep in mind.

In order to function properly, it is important to keep in mind that the **Separate App Sound feature** requires the connection of a separate audio device. It is imperative that the primary audio output be used at all times for system noises to guarantee that important calls and notifications are not overlooked.

10. Remap the Bixby Button to Access the Power Menu

When you press and hold the Power button on your Samsung Galaxy S24 Ultra (or any other Galaxy phone from the most current generation), Bixby will be activated automatically. However, you have the ability to change it so that it brings up the option for turning off the power instead, and you can even add double-press actions such as accessing the Camera, Maps, Google Assistant, or any other app that is commonly used. This is how you can accomplish it:

- Firstly, launch the **Settings app** on your device.
- To access the Side Button option, navigate to the **Advanced Features menu** and pick it.
- Select the action that will be performed when the Side button is double-pressed as well as when it is pressed and held.

Samsung Galaxy S24 Ultra User's Manual

- Double-pressing the button allows you to select Quick Launch camera, Samsung Wallet quick access, or Open app (you can select the app that you want to use).
- Switch from the Wake Bixby (default) menu to the Power off menu by pressing and holding the button.
- It is all that. Long-pressing the Side button will now allow you to enter the menu for turning off the device.

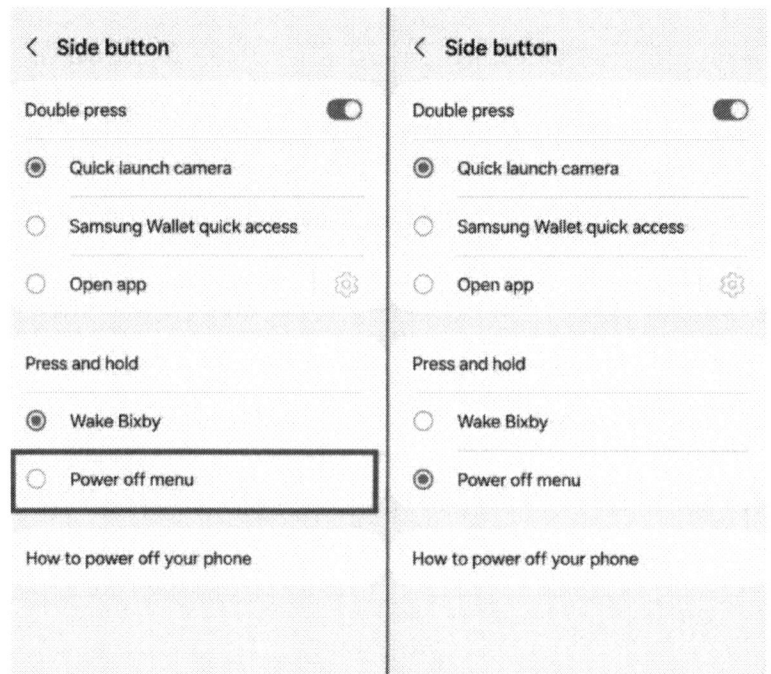

Let's say that you would like to keep Bixby's capabilities, you can still power down your Galaxy S24 Ultra in one of three ways: by tapping the Power button located in the quick panel, by telling Bixby to "turn off the phone," or by pressing and holding the Side and Volume down buttons in order to enter the power menu.

It is possible to set up a shortcut that allows you to access Google Assistant by double-pressing the button, for those who prefer it to Bixby. You may also remap the button by using third-party applications or by creating a Bixby routine to launch Assistant with the Side key (this requires the Routines+Goodlock module). Both of these options are available to you.

11. Switch to Dark Mode

Using the Samsung Galaxy S24 series, switching to Dark Mode takes advantage of the AMOLED displays that are available on the device. These displays have the ability to turn off individual pixels in order to display true blacks, which results in a lower battery usage compared to lighter colors.

Enabling Dark Mode not only helps to preserve the life of the battery but also alleviates eye strain, which is especially beneficial in low-light environments. In order to activate it, this is how:

- Activate the Settings application on your Samsung Galaxy S24 Ultra device.
- After navigating to Display, choose the Dark Mode option.

- The Dark Mode settings may be accessed by tapping on Dark Mode settings, enabling "Turn on as scheduled," and then choosing the desired timings for the Dark Mode to be activated.

When you switch to Dark Mode, the wallpaper on your home screen and lock screen will be subdued. Adapting this setting requires you to follow these steps:

- Navigate to the **Settings menu**.
- Then, choose the **wallpaper and style.**
- Disable the "Dim wallpaper when Dark mode is on.

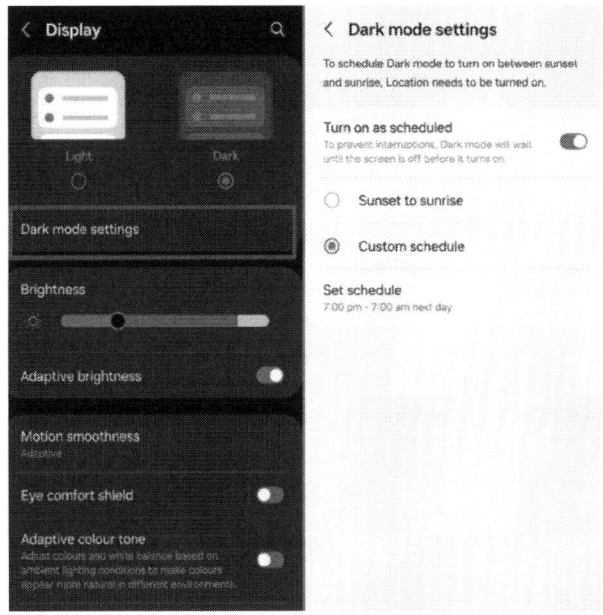

If you follow these steps, the display on your Samsung Galaxy S24 Ultra will be optimized for Dark Mode, which will improve both the battery life and the user's comfort, particularly in low-light conditions.

12. Use Advanced Battery Protection Features

The Galaxy S24 series introduces improved battery protection features using One UI 6.1, which is available for download. In the past, consumers were only able to top off their battery at 85%. Now, you can enjoy more precise control over the charging behavior of your phone, which will protect the health of its battery over time:

- To protect your battery, go to Settings > Battery > Battery Protection.
- Set the function to active and choose the level of security that best suits your needs.

I. When the battery reaches 100%, the charging process will stop, and it will resume when the battery reaches 95%.
II. In order to extend the lifespan of the battery, the maximum charge is stopped at 80%.
III. It charges the battery to 80% and then progressively tops it up to 100% based on usage patterns, such as your sleep schedule. This feature is quite similar to the Adaptive Charging feature that is available on the Google Pixel smartphone.

It is recommended that individuals who have a consistent charging habit, such as plugging in at night and unplugging in the morning, use the Adaptive mode. Users who have varying charging patterns should choose either the Basic or Maximum option, based on the frequency of their usage and their concern for the longevity of their battery.

13. Disable App Suggestions in the Recents Menu

There is a possibility that you will discover a section of app suggestions underneath the list of recently used applications when you visit the menu for recent apps in order to switch to the most recent app you used or to clear the list. The menu may become cluttered as a result of this, and it may not be useful to some people. You may disable the app suggestions that appear in the recent applications menu by following these steps:

- When you want to access the menu of recently used apps, swipe up from the navigation bar.
- Select **Settings** by tapping the three dots located in the upper-right corner of the screen.
- Using the **Recents app menu,** which is available on devices such as the Samsung Galaxy S24 Ultra running OneUI 6.1, turn off the option that is labeled "Show recommended apps..

Once you have completed these steps, the app suggestions will be removed from the screen that displays the most recent apps.

14. Unlock the Full Potential of Your S24 Ultra with S-Pen Air Actions

Using the S-Pen on your Samsung Galaxy S24 Ultra, which features user-friendly Air Actions, you will have a flawless experience controlling the device. You can effortlessly manage your phone, open applications, adjust the playback of music, look through images, and do much more without ever touching the display. All of this can be accomplished only through the use of simple gestures.

Using the S-Pen in conjunction with your Samsung Galaxy S24 Ultra opens up a whole new world of interaction possibilities through the use of Air Actions. To make full use of its features, proceed with the following steps:

- **Accessing Applications:** To quickly access the Camera application, remove the S-Pen from its slot and press and hold the button on the S-Pen. Depending on your preferences, you can personalize this action by going to Settings > Advanced Features > S Pen > Air Actions > Press and Hold Pen Button, and then selecting the application that you want to use.
- **App-Specific Functions:** Learn about Air Actions that are specifically designed for

each individual app. Changing the camera modes, for example, can be accomplished by pressing and holding the pen button, and then flipping left or right respectively. Similarly, you can navigate around your gallery by switching between left and right arrows.

- **Exploring Air Actions**: To investigate the Air Actions that are accessible for a particular application, you must first launch the application and then touch on the S-Pen icon that is displayed on the screen. It will be presented with a list of activities that are supported.
- **Customizing Actions**: The process of customizing actions involves going to Settings > Advanced Features > S Pen > Air Actions and selecting the app icon that you want to use. This allows you to tailor Air Actions to satisfy your preferences for each individual app.
- **Anywhere Actions:** Take advantage of several control options with Air Actions, which

can be accessed from any location on your smartphone. You need only push the button on the side and then carry out the gesture that corresponds to it. This is a list of the default actions for anywhere.

I. To go back to the previous screen, you need to draw a letter 'C' in the air.
II. Locate a 'Ɔ' to gain access to the most current applications.
III. If you want to return to the home screen, you can do so by performing a flick gesture that is similar to a "E'.
IV. Make a 'U' with your finger to activate Smart Select, which allows you to take screenshots.
V. When you want to enable Screen Write, shake the S-Pen.

Take note that in order to guarantee precise gesture recognition, you should hold the S-Pen in a parallel position to the ground while operating Air Actions.

Through the seamless integration of S-Pen Air Actions on the Samsung Galaxy S24 Ultra, you can take your smartphone experience to the next level.

15. Gain an Understanding of the Power of Galaxy AI

Learn about the cutting-edge Galaxy AI capabilities that have been implemented into the Samsung Galaxy S24 series. These features combine on-device processing with cloud processing in a fluid manner to transform the way you interact with your smartphone. Discover the necessary artificial intelligence capabilities that are waiting for you on the S24 Ultra:

On the Samsung Galaxy S24 Ultra, the Galaxy AI features include:

- **Live Translate for Calls**: Live Translate Call helps to break down barriers caused by linguistic differences by providing real-time translation of phone conversations for both parties involved.

- **Interpreter Mode**: It allows you to instantly translate speech into your favorite language and vice versa. This mode may be accessed from the quick settings panel, making it possible to communicate easily in situations that involve multiple languages.
- **Browsing Assist Summarize & Translate**: Your web browsing experience will be completely transformed with the help of the Browsing Assist Summarize & Translate feature, which is integrated into the Samsung Internet browser and features capabilities to summarize and translate webpages using artificial intelligence.
- **Note Assist:** The Samsung Notes app includes a feature called Note Assist, which is designed to improve productivity by providing artificial intelligence-driven capabilities such as note summarization, formatting, language translation, and word checking respectively.
- **Writing Assist for Messages**: You can improve the quality of your messaging experience by

using writing aid driven by artificial intelligence. This assistance will provide ideas for adjusting the tone of your messages, correcting your spelling and grammar, and translating your messages seamlessly across a variety of messaging platforms.

- **Transcribe Assist:** The Recorder app has a feature called Transcribe Assist, which allows users to convert speech recordings into text transcripts and summaries. This feature makes it easier to examine and translate audio content.
- **Generative Edit in Photos:** Unleash your creativity with Generative Edit in Photos, which enables dynamic editing of photos such as object removal, resizing, background adjustment, and angle correction.

This feature is driven by powerful artificial intelligence algorithms.

Samsung Galaxy S24 Ultra User's Manual

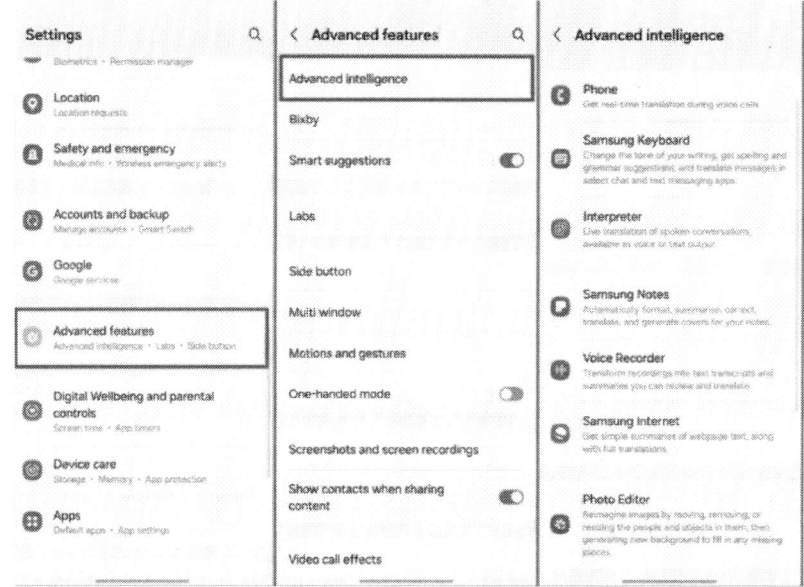

Accessing these game-changing capabilities on your Samsung Galaxy S24 Ultra is a simple and straightforward process. Simply go to Settings > Advanced Features > Advanced Intelligence, and you will be able to access a whole new world of opportunities with Galaxy AI.

16. Make use of the Circle to Search feature.

Circle to Search is a revolutionary application that enhances your browsing experience by giving an advanced version of Google Lens. This application allows you to do searches right from the screen of your phone while remaining within the application you are currently using. The Galaxy S24 Ultra comes pre-installed with the Circle to Search functionality, which can be used right out of the box.

- Simply tapping and holding the Home button (on smartphones that have on-screen button navigation) or the Navigation bar found at the bottom (on devices that use gestures) is all that is required to use the Circle to Search feature.
- Perform a search by first drawing a circle around the thing you want to find on your screen using either your finger or an S-Pen, and then lifting your finger to begin the search.

It doesn't matter if you circle, scribble, or tap an item on your screen; Google Lens will immediately begin to retrieve relevant information from the internet based on the text or object that you have selected. It is possible to instantly determine the breed of a puppy that has been observed on

Instagram or to discover the location where you can acquire the fashionable shoes that your favorite designer is carrying.

17. Use Bixby Routines to Automate Your Samsung Galaxy Experience

Bixby Routines is a built-in feature on Samsung Galaxy phones that is comparable to Apple's Shortcuts app for iPhones. It provides smooth automation by carrying out activities or modifying settings based on a variety of triggers, including the time of day, location, battery state, and other factors.

During the time when you are retiring for the night, for example, your phone is able to automatically turn off 5G, activate Power Saving mode, enable Do Not Disturb, and carry out further tasks. In a similar vein, when you load the YouTube app on your device, you have the ability to effortlessly increase the volume, turn off notifications, and enable auto-rotation.

In order to make your Galaxy experience more unique, let's get started on the process of developing a Bixby routine. Following that, we will discuss some useful routines that you may implement to get your automation journey off to a good start.

- Proceed to the **Settings app** on your Galaxy S24 Ultra by navigating to it.
- Proceed to the "Routines" tab after gaining access to the "Modes and Routines" menu.
- The "Add Routine" (+) button may be found in the upper right corner of the screen.

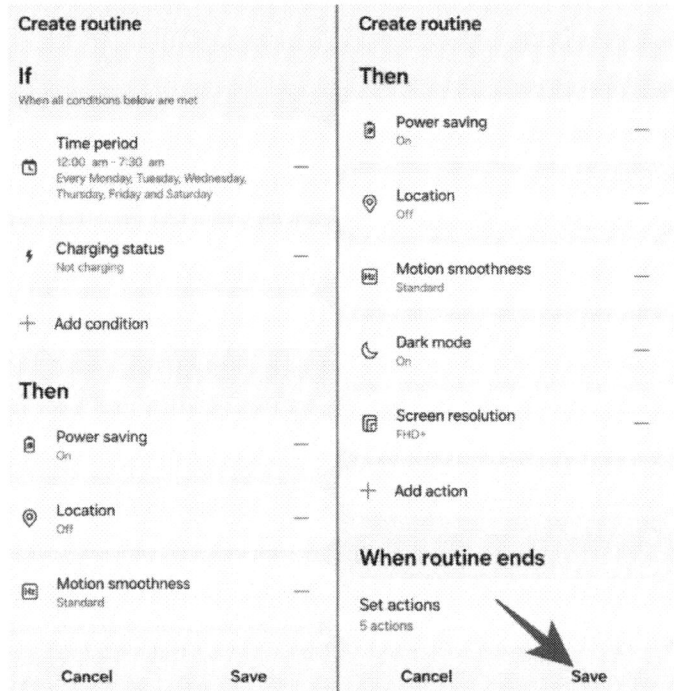

A few helpful Bixby routines that have been customized for your Galaxy S24 are as follows:

- **Preserve Battery Overnight:**

If — Time Period (set your bedtime), Charging Status: Not Charging

Then — Activate Power Saving Mode, Disable Location/5G/NFC/Bluetooth, Turn off Motion Smoothness, Enable Dark Mode.

- **Keep Screen Awake in Selected Apps:**

If — App Opened (e.g., YouTube or Netflix), Battery Level: 30% or higher

Then — Extend Screen Timeout to 10 minutes.

- **Switch to Vibrate Mode at Work:**

If — Location (set your workplace) or Wi-Fi (connect to workplace network)

Then — Switch Sound Mode to Vibrate.

- **Disable Fast Charging Overnight:**

If — Time Period (set your bedtime)

Then — Deactivate Fast Charging.

Through the implementation of these Bixby routines, your Galaxy experience will be streamlined, tasks will be automated, and efficiency will be enhanced without any difficulty.

18. Enable Notification History

Make sure you don't miss out on any vital notifications! If you have ever had the unfortunate experience of mistakenly deleting or clearing all of your notifications, you are familiar with the aggravation of the possibility of missing something vital. By your good fortune, the Notifications History feature of Android is here to assist you.

To guarantee that you will never again overlook an essential notification, follow these steps:

- You can access the advanced settings by going to Settings and selecting Notifications.
- Simply enable the feature by tapping on the Notification History option.
- Your Notification History will now be updated to include any notifications that you choose to ignore from the notification panel moving forward. In this manner, you will always have a backup to refer to even if you mistakenly delete their contents.

19. Enable Notification Categories

Beginning with Android 8.0 Oreo, Google made it possible for users to manage notifications for each app based on the category in which they fall. For instance, you have the option to stop Instagram notifications for comments, likes, live videos, IGTV, product announcements, and other types of content, while at the same time continuing to receive notifications for direct messages and phone calls.

On the other hand, Samsung has made the decision to disable this feature by default in One UI 6.1 on the Galaxy S24 Ultra. Following these steps will allow you to manually enable the option in your settings, which will allow you to reclaim control over your notifications with more degrees of granularity:

Samsung Galaxy S24 Ultra User's Manual

- Go to the Settings menu, and then pick the **Notifications option.**
- Go to the bottom of the page and select the **Advanced settings option.**
- Toggle the option for "Manage notification categories for each app..

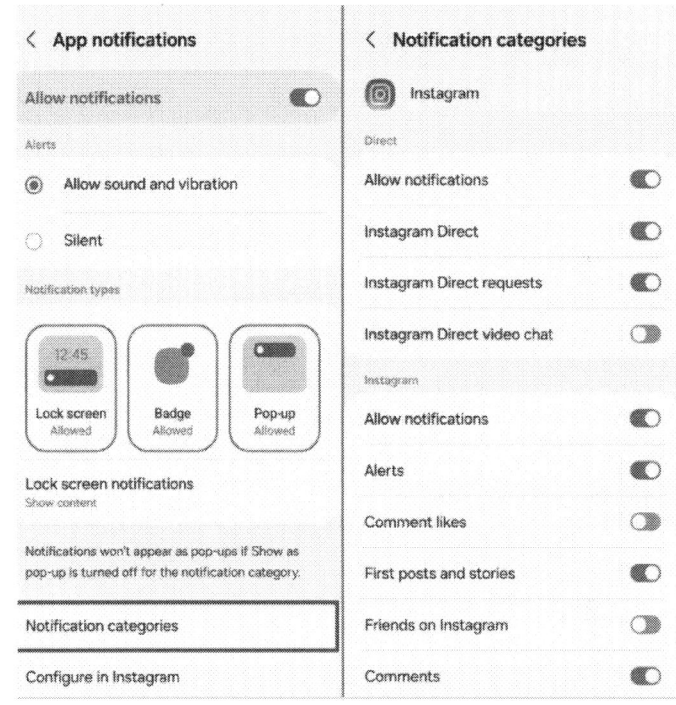

After the feature has been activated, you will find a new option titled "Notification categories" inside the Notifications section of the app's information page. In this section, you will have the ability to select which types of notifications you would want to receive alerts for and which ones you would rather not receive notifications for. This functionality helps to streamline your notifications, ensuring that you only receive the ones that are most relevant to you while minimizing excessive clutter from appearing on your screen.

20. Increasing the Capabilities of the Samsung Galaxy S24 Ultra to Support Offline Searching

In a manner comparable to those of Apple and Google, Samsung provides a **SmartThings Find network** that is intended to assist in the recovery of Galaxy devices that have been misplaced. Activating this option prior to purchasing your Galaxy S24 Ultra is something that we strongly recommend doing. Taking this action makes your phone discoverable by other Galaxy devices that are connected to the internet, even while it is not connected to the internet.

In addition, your Galaxy S24 Ultra is able to assist in the process of scanning for nearby missing devices, which may include other Galaxy phones as well as wearables that are compatible with it, such as earrings and watches. This functionality is accessible when offline finding is enabled on both devices and your S24 Ultra was the most recent device to which they were connected (with the exception of phones and SmartTags, which are able to connect to the SmartThings Find network directly).

To enable it, follow these steps:

- To access the **Security and Privacy settings**, navigate to the **Settings menu.**
- After that, choose **Lost Device Protection** on your device.
- Allow this phone to be located, Send latest location, and Offline Finding are all configuration options that should be enabled.
- You can verify your choice by hitting the Turn On button.

You may use either the **SmartThings app or the SmartThings Find website** to locate your Galaxy S24 Ultra in the event that it is misplaced. Additionally, you can use any of these to remotely ring or wipe it, which is a tool that complements Google's Find My Device feature.

Also, take note that Samsung offers a choice to activate offline locating during the first setup process of the phone. In the event that you have misplaced your device and are unable to recollect activating it through the settings, it is highly probable that you activated it during the initial setup process. Consequently, another viable choice is to make an effort to discover your gadget by making use of **Samsung Find.**

21. Optimal Good Lock Customizations for Your Galaxy S24 Ultra.

Do you want to customize your Galaxy S24 Ultra as soon as possible? You are in for a real treat with the Samsung Good Lock app, which gives you the ability to install mini-apps that offer a variety of changes, features, and additions in addition to the regular One UI adjustments.

Through the use of Good Lock, you are able to significantly alter the design of the quick panel, personalize the clock on your lock screen, modify the settings of the S-Pen, investigate new themes, enhance the ability to navigate between apps and multitask, and a great deal more.

To get started, all you need to do is transfer the **Good Lock application** from the Samsung Store onto your device.

To begin using the Good Lock app on your Galaxy S24 Ultra, your first step is to follow these steps:

- **The process of installation:**
I. The Good Lock app may be downloaded from the Samsung Store and installed.
II. Select the number of mini-modules that you want. Some of them will be installed as standard apps and will show up in your app

drawer, while others will be accessible directly from the interface of the Good Lock app.

- **Exploring the Good Lock:**
I. There are two primary categories of customization modules that are available through Good Lock: "Make up" and "Life up."
II. In contrast to "Life up," which focuses on practical changes and productivity tools, "Make up" is primarily concerned with visual customization, which includes the addition of themes and the modification of the overall appearance and feel.

Here are some of the Good Lock modules that are recommended:

- **LockStar:** You can personalize both your lock screen and your always-on display with LockStar. In addition to adding widgets and applying dynamic backdrop effects, you may change the font, color, and style of the clock.

- **NavStar:** You can customize your navigation bar with NavStar. Modify the order of the buttons, alter their look, and enable alternative swipe gestures. It is also possible to conceal the navigation bar.
- **QuickStar:** Simply update the user interface of your quick panel. Make changes to the layout, tile size, transparency, and colors, and add shortcuts that need a double tap.
- **Routines:** Bixby Routines can be improved with the addition of additional triggers and features, such as button triggers, touch macros, and interaction with the S-Pen under the Routines+ feature.
- **Camera Assistant:** The Camera Assistant is designed to enhance your experience with the camera by providing capabilities such as Auto HDR, picture smoothing, and faster shutter speed functionality.

- **RegiStar:** It allows you to personalize your home screen for Settings, reorganize or hide choices, and define custom actions for activities such as pressing and holding the side key and back-tapping.
- **Sound Assistant:** It allows you to activate features such as simultaneous audio playback and voice changer effects, as well as set separate volume levels for each app, configure the volume panel, and set the volume level.

Samsung Galaxy S24 Ultra User's Manual

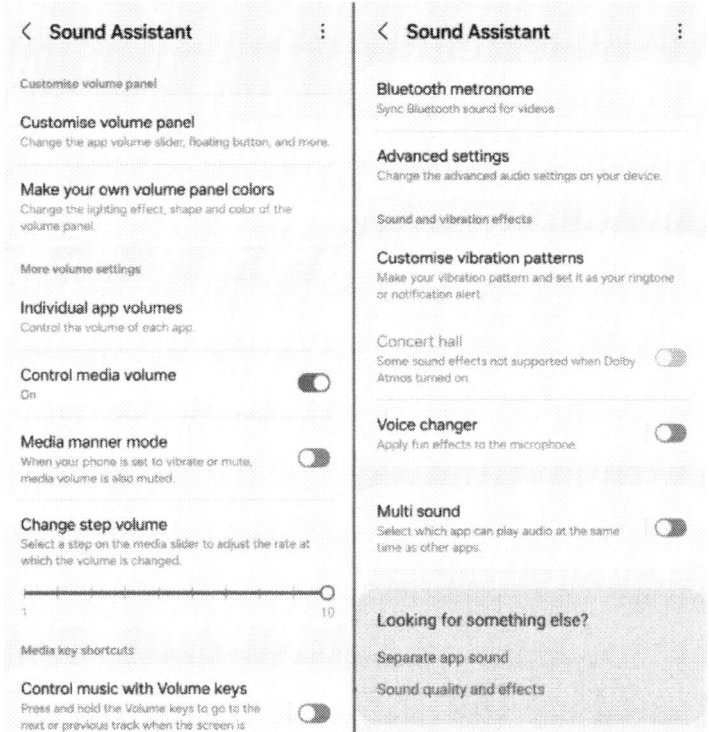

By making use of these customizations for Good Lock, you will be able to really personalize your Galaxy S24 Ultra to meet your tastes and improve the overall quality of your user experience.

CHAPTER FIFTEEN

Android 14 new updates with S24 Ultra

One UI 6.0, the most recent user interface that has been developed specifically for the Samsung Galaxy S24 Ultra and is based on Android 14, has been released by Samsung. The purpose of this update is to improve the overall level of satisfaction experienced by users by introducing a multitude of new features, enhancements, and customization possibilities.

In order to make One UI 6.0 available to all users and to extend its compatibility to devices that meet the requirements, the deployment of the software has begun. Those who are anxious to experience the most recent advancements can download and install One UI 6.0 on their Samsung Galaxy S24 Ultra smartphone by following the basic steps which will discussed as follows.

What is Samsung Android Update?

The introduction of new versions of the Android operating system that are specifically designed for Samsung Galaxy smartphones and tablets is what is meant by the term "Samsung Android (One UI) update." In most cases, these upgrades include increases to performance, patches to security vulnerabilities, bug repairs, and occasionally the introduction of new features and improvements respectively. The purpose of these updates is to provide consumers with the most recent software improvements and to ensure that their devices continue to be up to date and secure. Samsung provides these updates on a frequent basis.

Over-the-air (OTA) distribution is a frequent method for Samsung Android upgrades, which means that customers will receive a notification on their devices as soon as an update is made available. Users are then able to proceed with downloading and installing the update directly from the settings menu of their respective devices. Additionally,

Samsung may also deliver updates using its desktop software, which is known as Samsung Smart Switch. This software gives consumers the ability to update their devices directly from their computers.

In order to ensure optimal performance, security, and compatibility with the most recent applications and services, it is essential for customers to ensure that their Samsung devices are always updated with the most recent version of Android software.

How to Update Android 14 (One UI 6.0) on Samsung Galaxy S24 Ultra

The process of updating the operating system on the Samsung Galaxy S24 Ultra to Android 14 (One UI 6.0) is normally uncomplicated and consists of a few short steps. A general guide is provided below:

Step 1: Check for Updates

- Launch the "Settings" application on your Samsung Galaxy Mobile device.

- Go to the bottom of the page and select "Software update..
- You can check for available updates by selecting "Download and install" from the menu.

Step 2: Download Updates

Let us assume that an update is available, your mobile device will notify you to download it.

As updates can be rather substantial and require a significant amount of data, you should make sure that you have a reliable internet connection, preferably one that is Wi-Fi.

Step 3: Install any available updates

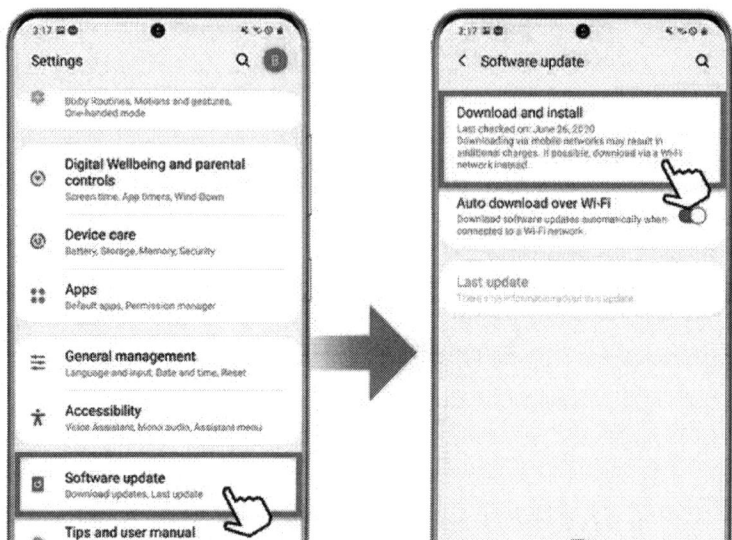

Following the completion of the download, you will need to select "Install now" in order to begin the process of installation.

To complete the installation, it is possible that your phone may need to be restarted.

Step 4: Automatic Updates

- Navigate to the "Software update" options in order to activate automatic updates.

- The option to "Download updates automatically" can be enabled by tapping on it and then toggling the switch.
- It is expected that the process of updating your Samsung Galaxy S24 Ultra will go well if you strictly adhere to these guidelines.

How to Update Android 14 (One UI 6.0) on Samsung Galaxy S24 Ultra using Odin

Using the Samsung Odin flash tool, which is a desktop application, to update your Samsung Galaxy phone is yet another feasible approach. In order to manually flash firmware into the Samsung Galaxy S24 Ultra, the following procedures need to be followed in order to upgrade the device:

This comprehensive guide will teach you how to flash Samsung stock firmware using the Odin tool.

Step 1: Back Up Your Data

It is essential to create a backup of all of your essential data before making any modifications to the software on your device. This includes creating copies of your images, videos, contacts, applications, and any other files that you wish to keep. For this purpose, you can make use of the backup tools that are integrated into Samsung devices or third-party applications.

Step 2: Download the necessary firmware files.

Obtain the most recent version of Android 14 (One UI 6.0) firmware that is customized for your particular Samsung Galaxy S24 Ultra phone model (SM-S928B, SM-S928B/DS, SM-S928U, SM-S928U1, SM-S928W, SM-S928N, SM-S9280, SM-S928E, SM-S928E/DS) from reputable suppliers such as SamMobile or SamFw.

In addition, make sure that you download and install the most recent version of Odin, which is a utility that runs on Windows and is used to flash firmware on Samsung devices.

Step 3: Obtain the Firmware Files

The firmware files that you have downloaded should be extracted, and the extensions that are frequently used are .tar and .tar.md5.

Step 4: Enable USB Debugging and Developer Options.

Make sure that your device is enabled with Developer Options, USB Debugging, and OEM Unlock before proceeding with the downgrade. Take the following actions:

- Locate the "Settings" menu and then select "About phone" on your Samsung Galaxy phone.
- To activate Developer Options, you must first tap on the "Build number" seven times.
- Navigate back to the main settings menu, select "Developer options," and then turn on "USB debugging.

Step 5: Install Samsung USB Drivers

It is necessary to download and install the official Samsung USB drivers on your computer in order to permit contact between your computer and your Samsung Galaxy device while the downgrading procedure is being carried out.

Step 6: Download and uninstall Odin

Discover a reliable site that offers the most recent version of Odin, and then download it. The Odin tool should be extracted to a specific location on your computer.

Step 7: Put the phone into download mode by booting it up.

Putting your device into Download Mode is the first step in the process of flashing the firmware:

- Make sure that your device is turned off.
- Maintain simultaneous pressure on the Volume Down button, the Bixby button, and the Power button.

- In order to access Download Mode, you will need to click the Volume Up button when a warning screen shows.

Step 8: Connect the phone to the computer.

Use a USB cord to establish a connection between your Samsung Galaxy phone and your computer.

Step 9: Launch the Odin Flash Tool.

You should start Odin on your computer and check to see if it recognizes your device. There ought to be a notification that says "Added!" displayed in the log pane.

Step 10: Select Firmware Files

To choose the firmware files that you extracted earlier, go to Odin and click on the buttons that correspond to BL, AP, CP, and CSC.

Step 11: Begin the process of flashing the firmware

In Odin, when you have checked and rechecked all of the options, click **the Start button.** It is now time to begin the process of flashing the firmware.

Step 12: Completion

When the process of flashing the firmware is finished, Odin will display a message that reads "Pass!" to indicate that the process was successful. The Samsung Galaxy phone you are using will then do an automatic restart.

Step 13: Configure Your Mobile Device

To finish the initial setup procedure when your phone has restarted, you will need to follow the instructions that appear on the screen.

Step 14: Factory Reset (Optional)

Performing a factory reset is an optional step that can be used to address any compatibility issues that may arise after downgrading:

- First and foremost, make sure that your device is turned off.
- In order to activate Recovery Mode, simultaneously press and hold the Volume Up button, the Bixby button, and the Power button.
- With the use of the volume buttons, navigate to the "Wipe data/factory reset" option, and then choose it by simultaneously pressing the Power button.
- Verify that the factory reset was successful, and then wait for the process to finish. Try restarting your device.

In the end;

In conclusion, there are a number of different ways to upgrade Android on Samsung Galaxy phones. These techniques include manual firmware flashing with Odin, over-the-air upgrades, and Samsung Smart Switch. Making sure that the operating system on your device is always up to date is essential if you want to improve its performance, stability, and security. By carefully following the instructions and making sure that you are using the appropriate firmware for your device model, you may avoid any difficulties that may arise. It is imperative that you create a backup of your vital data before engaging in any activity involving firmware flashing or upgrading.

CHAPTER SIXTEEN

Considering an Upgrade: Samsung Galaxy S24 Ultra vs. S23 Ultra

There is a plethora of options available in the premium Android market, which includes a multitude of flagship models that are distinguished by their outstanding performance, brilliant displays, attractive designs, and cameras that are comparable to those found in DSLRs. Within this group, the Galaxy S series stands out on a constant basis, and the most recent addition, the Galaxy S24 Ultra, continues to uphold the high standards that were established by its predecessors.

Artificial intelligence (AI) was the main attraction at this year's Samsung Unpacked presentation, which heralded huge improvements in the way that we interact with our devices. The Samsung Galaxy S24

Ultra emerges as one of the most intriguing and feature-rich Android devices of 2024, and it does it in a number of different ways. Nevertheless, the question that remains is whether or not it provides sufficient benefits to encourage owners of the Galaxy S23 Ultra to upgrade.

For those who are interested in learning more about the Galaxy S24 Ultra's improvements over its predecessor, the following is an exhaustive summary of the information that you need to be aware of.

Galaxy S24 Ultra vs. S23 Ultra: design

Despite the passage of time, Samsung continues to follow a strategy that is comparable to that of Apple, which is to introduce new flagship models with only minor modifications to their architecture. In comparison to its predecessor, the Galaxy S22 Ultra, which, when Samsung united the two series, inherited the design language of the Galaxy Note

20 Ultra, the Galaxy S23 Ultra received just minor improvements.

In a similar vein, the most recent generation, the Galaxy S24 Ultra, has the same look and feel as its predecessor, with only a few minor design adjustments. Notable among the modifications is the utilization of a titanium frame, which has taken the place of the harder aluminum alloy that was previously utilized. This shift seems to be a reflection of Apple's decision to incorporate titanium in the chassis of the iPhone 15 Pro. Even though Samsung asserts that this modification makes the gadget more durable, there is still a lack of evidence that can be considered concrete to demonstrate major improvements. On the other hand, the formerly chrome-finished frame of the Galaxy S23 Ultra is predicted to be more scratch-resistant than the titanium frame, which features a warmer texture and is expected to be more resistant to scratches. Furthermore, the straighter edges lead to a more firm grasp, which is another advantage.

The display on the Galaxy S24 Ultra has been redesigned to be flatter, which is another visible change. According to Samsung, the reduction in edge curvature can increase reading and productivity, despite the fact that it does not completely eliminate the curvature. Although it has caused some users to express their disagreement, this modification improves the writing experience with the S Pen and does not dramatically impact the viewing area.

The Galaxy S24 Ultra utilizes the most recent iteration of Corning's Gorilla Glass, which is referred to as Gorilla Glass Armor. This particular version of Gorilla Glass guarantees a scratch resistance that is four times greater and a reduction in reflection that is up to seventy-five percent.

In spite of these alterations, the overall proportions of the Galaxy S24 Ultra have been subjected to some modest revisions, which have resulted in a device that is marginally taller and narrower in comparison to its predecessor. The transition to titanium does not have a substantial impact on the weight of the gadget, as it weighs only one gram less than the previous model, despite the fact that it is slightly thicker than the previous model. On the other hand, the majority of people might not notice the variations in size and weight if they do not make a direct comparison.

Alongside the black variety that is already available, Samsung has introduced new color possibilities such as yellow, gray, and violet. These new color options are in addition to the updated frame and display. In addition, Samsung's website offers a selection of colors that are not available anywhere else.

In addition to the changes made to the frame and display, the Galaxy S24 Ultra primarily keeps the design aspects that were present in its predecessor. These elements include the fragmented circular rings for the rear cameras, a flattened frame for increased grip, and the slot for the S Pen. Although the positioning of buttons has not altered, Samsung has begun using recycled thermoplastics in their production process, which accounts for 10% of the total. There have been some small tweaks made to the internal components, notably the cameras, which will be covered in further detail in subsequent sections.

Galaxy S24 Ultra vs. S23 Ultra: display

Previously noted, the Galaxy S24 Ultra comes with a display that has been upgraded. With a peak luminance of 2,600 nits, the display of the Galaxy S24 Ultra is substantially brighter than the display of the Galaxy S23 Ultra, which had a peak luminance of 1,750 nits. This is in addition to the physical modifications that have been made to the panel, the most notable of which is the strengthened Gorilla Armor glass that has been added for improved management of reflections. Taking into consideration that "peak brightness" refers to the highest luminosity of each individually lit pixel, which is especially noticeable while viewing HDR content, it is essential to keep this in mind.

In addition, Samsung does not provide the brightness specs for other modes, despite the fact that other metrics, such as normal brightness and High Brightness Mode (HBM), indicate the maximum brightness of the panel as a whole. The latter mode can be activated manually or in high ambient light settings, such as sunshine. However, in our experience, we have discovered that the screen is sufficiently viewable even on bright days when the brightness is set to its maximum. Furthermore, the Adaptive Brightness setting ensures that the S24 Ultra maintains the ideal brightness levels over time without causing any unnecessary oscillations.

When compared to the model from the previous year, there are not many noticeable alterations, with the exception of the appearance and brightness. This continuity demonstrates Samsung's dedication to preserving what has shown to be both successful and efficient. The Galaxy S24 Ultra demonstrates Samsung's continued proficiency in display technology, which is evident in the company's long-standing tradition of supplying displays for a variety of flagship phones, including iPhones and OnePlus smartphones.

This LTPO display, which was formerly marketed under the name "Dynamic AMOLED 2X," features a variable refresh rate that ranges from 1 to 120Hz. It is designed to synchronize with the frame rate of the content that is being presented in order to eliminate tearing or errors.

In addition, the display continues to support the full DCI-P3 color gamut and maintains a resolution that is equivalent to or higher than Quad HD+, consistent with previous releases. Dolby Vision compatibility is not included in the Galaxy S24 Ultra, despite the fact that it continues to support the HDR10+ standard. On the other hand, the increased brightness of the panel might alleviate some of the worries that have been raised about its ability to compete with less expensive panels that supported Dolby Vision in the previous generation.

Galaxy S24 Ultra vs. S23 Ultra: performance

The physical capabilities of the Galaxy S24 Ultra are the primary factor that differentiates it from the Galaxy S23 Ultra. It was the first global release to have this cutting-edge chip, and it was powered by the Qualcomm Snapdragon 8 Gen 3 chipset, which was introduced in October of 2023.

The Snapdragon 8 Gen 3 went through a number of important changes, most notably in the configuration of the central processing unit cores, with the intended purpose of improving performance. Qualcomm claims that the total performance of the Snapdragon 8 Gen 2 has improved by thirty percent compared to the previous generation. In addition, the graphics performance has been significantly improved by as much as 25 percent, which promises an improved gaming experience. An effort has been made by Samsung in conjunction with a number of game studios to encourage the widespread implementation of ray tracing in Android games. It is worth noting that Diablo Immortal, Racing Master, Arena Breakout, and Night Crows are among the games that were among the first to feature ray tracing.

The Galaxy S24 Ultra features special innovations, one of which is a vapor cooling chamber that is 90 percent larger than the one found in its predecessor, the S23 Ultra. This further enhances the performance of devices. Because of this expansion, heat can be dissipated more effectively during activities that require a lot of effort. As an additional point of interest, all storage options, ranging from 256GB to 1TB, now come standard with 12GB of RAM. During intense gaming sessions or benchmarking stress tests, the Galaxy S24 Ultra is able to handle demanding activities without overheating, which is a significant advantage in terms of practicality.

Not only does the Snapdragon 8 Gen 3 processor bring a staggering 98% boost in neural processing capabilities, but it also introduces incredible raw computing power. This improvement makes it possible to execute operations involving artificial intelligence directly on the device, so minimizing the dependency on data centers that are hosted in the cloud. In order to take advantage of this development, Samsung has incorporated generative artificial intelligence elements into the Galaxy S24 series. Functionalities of AI that are noteworthy include:

- **Live Translate**: This feature, known as Live Translate, enables real-time translation during calls and also includes live transcription, all of which is performed locally on the platform.
- **Chat Assist:** It has the capability to provide text production and real-time translation in third-party messaging applications such as

WhatsApp or Google Messages, in addition to adjusting the tone of the message.

- **Note Assist:** Within the Samsung Notes app, the Note Assist feature makes use of artificial intelligence to summarize notes and draw conclusions that are meaningful.
- **Transcript Assist:** Audio recordings or voice notes can be automatically transcribed with the help of Transcript Assist.
- **Circle to search:** Users are able to search for certain material by just circling it on the screen, which is made possible by the Circle to Search feature.
- The upcoming upgrade for Android Auto will make it possible to summarize messages and notifications while an individual is driving.

There is a possibility that these artificial intelligence functions will be available on other Android smartphones because they are dependent on Google's Gemini Nano machine learning model. In an upcoming update, Samsung intends to bring these functions to the Galaxy S23 Ultra version of the device.

The following section on cameras will also provide a comprehensive discussion of the many picture altering features and applications that are driven by artificial intelligence.

Galaxy S24 Ultra vs. S23 Ultra: battery and charging

Following in the footsteps of its predecessor, the Galaxy S23 Ultra, the Galaxy S24 Ultra keeps its battery capacity at 5,000 mAh. Customers who are concerned about the environment should be aware that Samsung has included recycled cobalt in the battery of the Galaxy S24 Ultra, which accounts for fifty percent of the total. It is possible that this modification will not necessarily result in noticeable improvements to the battery life of the phone, despite the fact that it highlights Samsung's dedication to being more environmentally responsible.

Support for cable charging speeds of up to 45 watts is still available for the Galaxy S24 Ultra, which means that it can continue to be used for charging purposes. In addition, wireless charging is accessible at 15W with chargers that are certified or branded by Samsung, and it is available at 5W with any other Qi-qualified accessories. Additionally, the Galaxy S24 Ultra provides the convenience of reverse power sharing, which enables the charging of accessories such as Galaxy Buds or Galaxy Watch at a maximum power output of 3W.

No information has been provided by Samsung regarding whether the improved battery performance of the Galaxy S24 Ultra is due to the revised internals or any artificial intelligence algorithms. On the other hand, according to our experience with Samsung's premium flagship phones, lengthy battery life continues to be one of the most notable qualities of these electronic devices. I would like to bring to your attention the possibility that there will be an initial adjustment phase during which the phone will optimize the performance of its battery. Consequently, even if the battery life seems to be below average at first, it is likely to drastically improve once a few charging cycles have been completed. Over the course of our testing, we were able to achieve up to five hours of intense screen usage, which included gaming and streaming video, with roughly fifty percent of the battery left by the end of the day.

Galaxy S24 Ultra vs. S23 Ultra: cameras

This year, the Samsung Galaxy S24 Ultra is prepared to win that title with its expanded capabilities, most notably an updated 200MP sensor in comparison to its predecessor, the Samsung Galaxy S23 Ultra, which stood out as one of the top camera phones in the previous year.

However, Samsung claims that the new sensor is sixty percent larger than the ISOCELL HP2 found in the Galaxy S23 Ultra, despite the fact that the company did not go into specifics during its lecture. This is expected to result in a significant improvement in low-light performance as well as an enhancement of optical image stabilization (OIS), which will reduce blurring that is caused by movement or shocks.

A new 5x periscopic telephoto sensor has been included, which is a major upgrade to the camera system. On paper, this may appear to be a step down from the 10x periscope that was featured on the Galaxy S23 Ultra. Nevertheless, Samsung is utilizing sophisticated artificial intelligence algorithms to optimize zoomed photos, which guarantees a smooth transition from 2x to 10x magnification. The Galaxy S24 Ultra uses a cropping approach rather than the conventional zooming method, which allows it to preserve image quality that is comparable to that of optical zoom. Samsung promises that this periscope function may achieve a zoom of up to one hundred times, and that it will produce clear photographs by utilizing generative artificial intelligence to improve details.

In the course of our investigation into the telephoto cameras of the Galaxy S24 Ultra and its predecessor, we came to the realization that this method, in general, yields remarkable outcomes. As a result of pixel cropping, there may be a minor drop in information when zooming in at 10 times the normal distance; nonetheless, the overall image quality is superior to that of the previous model, which results in photographs that are more visually pleasing.

The remaining sensors, such as the ultrawide sensor with 12 megapixels and the telephoto sensor with 10 megapixels and a magnification of three times, have not been altered. On the other hand, Samsung has included the artificial intelligence capabilities of the Snapdragon 8 Gen 3 in order to dramatically improve the performance of the camera.

The on-device artificial intelligence processing system of the Snapdragon 8 Gen 3 is referred known as the "ProVisual Engine," and it is utilized by the Galaxy S24 series to improve photographs in real time. Among these artificial intelligence features are image sharpening, reduction of shutter latency, and even the ability to propose modifications through a function called "Generative Edit," which is similar to the Google Pixel 8 series.

Additionally, Samsung has addressed issues with excessive high dynamic range (HDR) in photographs by developing Super HDR, which, prior to processing, provides a preview of photographs that contain HDR in the viewfinder. Consequently, users are able to alter the HDR settings in accordance with their preferences, and third-party applications like as Instagram are now able to capture HDR photographs or videos. HDR metadata, on the other hand, will not be recorded alongside the shot, in contrast to the Pixel 8, which will ensure that the image will seem the same across all screens.

It is possible that previous models, particularly the Galaxy S23 Ultra, will not be able to take use of these camera advances because a significant number of them are dependent on upgraded hardware, such as sensor and chip updates.

Galaxy S24 Ultra vs. S23 Ultra: software and updates

The most recent upgrade to Samsung's One UI, version 6, which is built on Android 14 and has substantial design enhancements across a variety of Galaxy S and A series smartphones, has begun rolling out. The fast settings panel has been refined, wallpaper-based theming has been improved, a new typeface has been added, and other improvements have been made as a result of this release, which marks a significant advancement of Samsung's unique Android interface.

The update to One UI 6 has already been implemented for the Galaxy S23 series, which includes the Ultra edition. This ensures that the Galaxy S24 Ultra will arrive with the most recent version of the software. Additionally, Samsung will be introducing new capabilities through the upgraded version of One UI, which will be pre-installed on the Galaxy S24 Ultra as well as other S24 variants.

Despite the fact that it is anticipated that many of these capabilities would ultimately be made available on earlier devices such as the Galaxy S23 series, Samsung has not yet discussed customizing tools that are comparable to the artificial intelligence-generated wallpapers found on the Pixel 8. Despite this, it is not out of the question that such capabilities could arise as the Android ecosystem continues to more embrace this trend.

Samsung is making similar pledges by promising seven years of Android version and security upgrades for the Galaxy S24 series. This news is in line with Google's declaration that the Pixel 8 series will receive firmware updates for a period of seven years. Despite being only one generation apart, the Galaxy S24 Ultra has a significant advantage over its predecessor, the Galaxy S23 Ultra, which will only receive three more Android version updates after Android 14. This durability distinguishes the Galaxy S24 Ultra from its predecessor.

Galaxy S24 Ultra vs. S23 Ultra: price and availability

Beginning at $1,300 for the 256GB option, the Galaxy S24 Ultra has been made available for purchase at major shops and carriers in the United States. When compared to the price that was initially set for the S23 Ultra, this is an increase of $100. Additional storage options include upgrades with capacities of 512 gigabytes and one terabyte, with prices of $1,420 and $1,660, each. Titanium Black, Titanium Gray, Titanium Violet, and Titanium

Yellow are some of the color options available, while Titanium Blue, Titanium Green, and Titanium Orange are hues that are only available because they are specific to this year.

It is now available for purchase at a price of $1,200 for those who are contemplating purchasing the Galaxy S23 Ultra; however, on third-party platforms such as Amazon and Walmart, excellent offers can be discovered. Our expectation is that additional price reductions for the S23 Ultra will be implemented in the not too distant future, following the launch of its successor.

Galaxy S24 Ultra vs. S23 Ultra: verdict

When compared to its predecessor, the Samsung Galaxy S24 Ultra is a substantial advancement. It features improved performance, a polished display, and updated cameras. The expanded software support that Samsung provides for the Galaxy S24 Ultra, on the other hand, is what actually differentiates it from the Galaxy S23 Ultra and makes it the more obvious pick. With a commitment to seven years of Android generation and security upgrades, the Galaxy S24 Ultra guarantees continuing software optimization and security until

Android 21. This is despite the fact that there may be constraints in the advancement of hardware, notably in the chipset.

If Samsung were to significantly lower the price of the Galaxy S23 Ultra, it would become a more tempting alternative in terms of value for money. This would be the only circumstance in which the Galaxy S23 Ultra could still be thought of as having an advantage over the Galaxy S24 Ultra. An additional alternative would be to obtain an alluring offer from a smaller retailer, possibly through a personal relationship. This would be another approach to influence the decision. In any other case, selecting the Galaxy S24 Ultra ensures that you will have quick access to newly developed artificial intelligence functions and that you will receive superior support in the years to come.

The necessity of upgrading to the Galaxy S24 Ultra, on the other hand, is very arguable if you currently have the Galaxy S23 Ultra and pride yourself on being its proud owner. The Galaxy S23 Ultra is still an exceptional Android device, and it is likely to benefit from the majority of the Galaxy AI features that were released with the Galaxy S24 Ultra. This is despite the fact that the S24 Ultra clearly delivers advances in terms of its technical capabilities.

CHAPTER SEVENTEEN

Troubleshooting

Using this detailed guide, you will be able to investigate potential solutions for more than sixteen typical problems that Samsung Galaxy S24 Ultra users encounter. Although it is possible that these problems are common across a variety of mobile devices, the primary focus of our attention is on addressing and explaining particular concerns that have been found with the Samsung Galaxy S24 Ultra 5G. Our group of knowledgeable professionals has thoroughly examined and suggested potential options in order to guarantee an efficient result. Ensure to take the time to read the chapter in its entirety before making any changes to the settings of your device. It contains information that will prove to be really helpful.

The Samsung Galaxy S24 Ultra provides a visually spectacular experience thanks to its 6.8-inch AMOLED Dot Drop display, which supports HDR10+, has a refresh rate of 120Hz, allows for 1 billion colors to be shown, and has a peak brightness of 2600 nits. This smartphone is able to support almost all Android games without any problems because it is equipped with a Snapdragon 8 Gen 3 chipset and operates on Android version 14 (One UI 6.1). Take stunning photographs with its 200-megapixel quadruple artificial intelligence camera array, which is supplemented by a 12-megapixel front-facing camera for capturing stunning selfies. With a powerful battery capacity of 5000 mAh, the Samsung Galaxy S24 Ultra ensures extended usage, enabling you to travel up to 2.5 days without the need to recharge the device. As an additional convenience, it also allows quick charging at 18 watts, which is noteworthy. Even though it weighs only 77 kg, it continues to be a favorite among people who are passionate about Samsung mobile phones.

Common troubleshooting issues and solutions

1. **Addressing the Camera Failed Issue on Galaxy S24 Ultra:**

First step: Restart Your Galaxy S24 Ultra:

If you encounter the "Camera Failed" error, perform a forced restart to refresh your phone's memory.

- Press and hold the Volume Down and Power buttons simultaneously until the Samsung logo appears.

Second step: Reset Camera App:

Resolve app-related issues by resetting the Camera app.

- Tap and hold the camera icon, select "App info," then navigate to "Storage."
- Clear cache and clear data to address potential app problems.

Third step: Factory Reset (Backup First!):

If software-related issues persist, consider a factory reset.

- Before proceeding, ensure to take a full backup of your phone.
- Perform a factory reset through the phone's settings.

Fourth step: Check for Software Updates:

Ensure your device is running the latest software version.

- Go to Settings > Software Update and download/install any available updates.

Fifth step: Wipe Cache Partition:

Eliminate potential conflicts caused by cached data by clearing the cache partition.

- Turn off your phone, then press Volume Up + Power to access the recovery menu.

- Navigate to "Wipe Cache Partition" and confirm the action.

Sixth step: Safe Mode:

Identify if a third-party app is causing the camera issue by booting your phone in Safe Mode.

- Press and hold the Power button, then tap on Safe Mode.
- Test the camera in Safe Mode and uninstall recently added apps if necessary.

Seventh step: Contact Samsung Support:

- If all else fails, seek assistance from Samsung Support for further diagnosis and resolution.
- They can help address potential hardware issues with your Galaxy S24 Ultra.

2. Resolving Unexpected Shutdowns on Samsung Galaxy S24 Ultra

Your Samsung Galaxy S24 Ultra may be experiencing sudden shutdowns, if you are experiencing them. It is possible that cookies and permissions are the root cause of this problem, which can manifest itself at any time. It could be the result of a bug or an infection with malware. If you want to address this issue, you might think about going to a Samsung service center in the area. There, skilled professionals will be able to use specialist software to both diagnose and fix the problem, so guaranteeing that your device will continue to function properly.

It is possible that your mobile device could sustain damage if it is unable to switch back on after being unexpectedly turned off. When this occurs, it is recommended that you seek assistance from a service station that is located nearby. Through the utilization of their software solutions, their specialists are able to address the underlying bug or virus problem, thereby restoring the functionality of your device.

In order to troubleshoot and perhaps resolve the issue with the Samsung Galaxy S24 Ultra having trouble shutting down, the following procedures can be taken:

- You can try using Force Start by pushing the Power button, the Volume Up button, and the Volume Down button all at the same time.
- It is recommended that you get professional assistance at the Samsung service station that is located closest to you if the problem continues to occur.
- Put your phone into Safe Mode so that you may locate and remove any software or applications that are causing you problems.
- Make an effort to perform a hard reset on your device if the issue continues to exist despite the actions described above.

Suppose that your mobile device has been subjected to physical damage, such as that which may have been caused by a fall, it is imperative that you have it inspected by a trained mobile repair professional who is able to evaluate and address any hardware issues that may have occurred.

In order to resolve the issue of the unexpected shutdown and ensure that your Samsung Galaxy S24 Ultra continues to function without any interruptions, you will need to follow these procedures and seek the proper assistance.

3. **Taking Measures to Address Concerns Regarding Overheating with the Samsung Galaxy S24 Ultra 5G**

Consider your Samsung Galaxy S24 Ultra 5G to be a superhero; even the most powerful heroes can experience excruciating pain when they are exerting themselves to their full potential. It is possible to overheat your phone by playing games or using it while it is charging, especially when the weather is warm. This is similar to the situation that occurs when a superhero is pushed to their limits. Fear not, however! We have the answer to maintain our superhero's cool and ensure that it is able to perform at its highest level. This is what you are able to do:

- **Avoid Charging Your Phone Excessively**: To avoid overcharging your phone, you could set an alarm to remind you to unplug it once it reaches 99% charge.
- **Make sure to do a system restart**: In some cases, a straightforward restart might work wonders in correcting difficulties related to overheating. In order to give your phone a new beginning, you should restart the system.
- **Remove the Cover from Your Phone**: While It Is Charging In order to reduce the amount of heat that is generated by your phone while it is charging, you should remove the cover from your phone.

- **Uninstall superfluous apps:** If your phone is operating in the background and contributing to overheating, you should remove any apps that are strange or superfluous from your device using the uninstall feature.
- **Limit charging time:** It is important to limit the amount of time that your phone is connected in for charging purposes. If you leave your phone plugged in for a lengthy period of time, it may become overheated.
- **Stop Running Background Apps**: If you want your phone to continue operating without any hiccups, you should stop running any background apps that aren't necessary and could be putting a drain on its resources.
- **Disable connectivity features**: In order to limit the amount of work that is placed on the hardware of your phone, you should temporarily disable connectivity features such as Wi-Fi, Bluetooth, and GPS while they are not being used.

- **Check for software updates:** You should check for software updates to ensure that the software on your phone is up to date. You may do this by checking for and installing any outstanding updates, as these updates may include remedies for issues related to overheating.

You will be able to help your Samsung Galaxy S24 Ultra 5G maintain peak performance while also keeping it cool and comfortable if you follow these guidelines. This will allow it to continue to perform like the superhero that it is!

4. Addressing Poor Battery Performance in Samsung Galaxy S24 Ultra – Effective Solutions

Have you noticed that your Samsung Galaxy S24 Ultra is suffering a quick depletion on its battery? Now that we have this problem under control, let's work together to find a solution.

Even though that it provides exceptional performance, the Snapdragon 662 chipset that is included in the Galaxy S24 Ultra might put a burden on the battery. This, in conjunction with other characteristics like as the super AMOLED Dot Drop Display, which boasts a refresh rate of 120 GHz and a peak brightness of 400 nits, can result in a rapid depletion of the battery. How to deal with it is as follows:

- **Monitor usage:** To conduct an accurate monitoring of your device's usage and screen time, navigate to the **Settings menu** and select **Battery.**
- **Manage Notifications:** Take steps to reduce clutter by turning off notifications for applications that aren't necessary. To simplify this process, navigate to the Settings menu and then select the Apps option.
- **Energy conservation:** Turning off Wi-Fi, Bluetooth, GPS, and mobile hotspots while they are not in use is an effective way to conserve energy through energy conservation.

- **Background Processes:** It is important to keep a close eye on the activities that are running in the background to ensure that no applications are stealthily eliminating your battery life.
- **Optimize settings:** To further increase the life of the battery, optimize the settings by turning off the auto-brightness feature and activating the power-saving mode.
- **Limiting Screen Time:** In order to maximize productivity, you should keep your screen time to less than one minute, particularly when you are not using it for vital purposes.
- **Updates to the Software**: It is important to check for official software updates on a regular basis in order to improve the performance of the system and fix any battery optimization issues.
- **Avoid Overcharging:** If you want your phone's battery to last longer, you can avoid overcharging it instead.

If the battery continues to deplete at a quick rate despite these attempts, you might want to consider resetting your phone. Also, if the issue continues to exist even after the device has been reset, it may be required to seek assistance from a mobile repair shop.

It is possible for you to properly handle the problem with the performance of the battery in your Samsung Galaxy S24 Ultra if you put these strategies into action.

5. Open any applications on the Samsung Galaxy S24 Ultra in a manner similar to a lazy load.

Have you become weary of the slow loading time of the applications on your Samsung Galaxy S24 Ultra, which is comparable to a sluggish loading process? This widespread problem, which frequently arises as a result of ineffective storage management and the utilization of inefficient applications and games, may be quite annoying for users.

On the other side, there is a remedy that can completely change the situation. By doing a **Hard Reset** on your Samsung Galaxy S24 Ultra 5G in a quick and efficient manner, you can reclaim the speed the device deserves.

You may take command of the performance of your device and put an end to the aggravation of delayed app launches. It's time to rediscover the speed that's always there.

Instructions on How to Deal with Slow App Openings on the S24 Ultra 5G:

When you use your Samsung Galaxy S24 Ultra, do you notice that the user interface is sluggish and that you experience lags? You have nothing to worry about because you will be able to easily solve this problem by following the methods that are outlined below. Despite the fact that this is a problem that frequently occurs in older mobile phones, if you are experiencing it on your device, it is most likely because the storage that is supported by RAM for running applications has reached its maximum capacity. Verify that your mobile device has a suitable amount of available ROM space. If not, you should think about deleting programs that aren't being used.

- Delete any applications that are not being used on your device.
- Be sure to switch to the default theme of the Samsung Galaxy S24 Ultra if you are using a theme that is not native to the device.
- Remove any applications that are used for garbage cleaning or antivirus protection.
- Reduce the amount of items in your storage space to roughly 80 percent if it is nearly full (around 90 percent).
- Avoid using launchers that are provided by third parties.
- If you have any antivirus software installed, remove it.

- Choose lighter versions of applications such as Facebook Lite, Twitter Lite, YouTube Go, and other similar apps.
- Lite versions of several applications, such as Facebook Lite, Twitter Lite, and others, should be taken into consideration. In addition, make sure that the software on your device as well as the applications you use are always up to date.

6. Concerns Regarding the Touchscreen on the Samsung Galaxy S24 Ultra

As a result of its remarkable quality and user interface experience, the display of the Samsung Galaxy S24 Ultra has garnered a lot of attention in the Android market. On the other hand, a number of customers have reported experiencing a bothersome issue that is referred to as the "ghost touch" issue. This is a situation in which the screen appears to respond on its own, as if a ghost were operating the device.

Steps to Take in Order to Fix Touchscreen Problems:

- A restart of your Samsung Galaxy S24 Ultra is the first step you should do in order to potentially cure any software hitches or temporary malfunctions.
- Take off the back cover and examine the touchscreen for any physical obstructions or inadvertent touch interference that could be affecting its performance.
- To prevent accidental touches from registering on the screen, you need enable the Accidental Touch Sensor function in the settings of your smartphone.
- Rebooting your Samsung Galaxy S24 Ultra will allow you to refresh its system and maybe repair any underlying software issues that may be causing the touchscreen issue.
- To achieve the best possible responsiveness from the touchscreen, navigate to the

settings menu of the device and make any necessary adjustments to the touch sensitivity settings.

- You can also execute a button combination by simultaneously pressing the power button, the volume up button, and the volume down button. This will allow you to perform a button combination that may assist in recalibration of the touchscreen.

- You should check for any available software patches and updates for your device, and if any are discovered, you should proceed to update your Samsung Galaxy S24 Ultra to the most recent version in order to fix any known flaws or glitches.

- In a similar manner, check for updates for all of the applications that are installed on your device and make sure that they are up to date. Outdated applications may be a contributing factor to touchscreen troubles.

There is a possibility that you will need to do a factory reset on your Samsung Galaxy S24 Ultra if the issue continues to exist after you have attempted the actions that have been recommended above. Before moving on to the next step, you should make sure that you have a backup of your data, as this step will delete all of the data and settings on your device.

You will be able to efficiently troubleshoot and resolve touchscreen issues on your Samsung Galaxy S24 Ultra if you follow these instructions. This will ensure that the user experience is fluid and responsive.

7. Problems with the Wi-Fi Connection on the Samsung Galaxy S24 Ultra

It is impossible to overestimate the importance of Wi-Fi in this day and age of digital technology, since it acts as a vital resource in situations where mobile data is unavailable. Therefore, it can be extremely frustrating to experience difficulties with the connectivity of Wi-Fi technology. The following is a detailed guide to addressing Wi-Fi connection issues that is specifically built for the Samsung Galaxy S24 Ultra. This guide was created with the understanding that uninterrupted internet access is extremely important.

To solve the problem, proceed with the following steps:

- Make sure that your device is attempting to connect to a Wi-Fi network by checking the Wi-Fi connection.
- In order to ensure that you are within the range of the Wi-Fi signal, it is necessary to verify the signal range.
- Restarting your phone will allow you to refresh the connectivity settings and may also repair any software issues that may have occurred.
- To ensure that your router is functioning properly and sending signals in the correct manner, it is important to perform a thorough inspection of its performance.

- If the problem continues, you should try to reset your mobile device to the settings that it had when it was first purchased.

If the issue continues to exist after you have completed the steps outlined above, proceed with the advanced troubleshooting steps that are listed below:

- Find the Wi-Fi Settings menu on your Samsung Galaxy S24 Ultra and navigate to it.
- Click the "View More" button to have access to further choices.
- The application programming interface should be changed from "DHCP" to "Statics" (Static IP).
- You should make an effort to connect to the Wi-Fi network of your choice.

Following these steps will allow you to successfully troubleshoot and resolve any issues that may arise with the Wi-Fi connectivity on your Samsung Galaxy

S24 Ultra, so ensuring that you will have uninterrupted access to the internet.

8. The fingerprint sensor on the Galaxy S24 Ultra is malfunctioning.

Several customers of the Galaxy S24 Ultra have raised concerns over the functioning of their fingerprint readers. Nevertheless, there are basic methods that can be implemented to remedy this issue:

Steps to Take in Order to Fix Issues with Fingerprint Sensors:

- Check to see if you are using the same finger that was registered during the setup process.
- Make sure the fingerprint sensor is free of any scratches or other damage.
- Through the settings on your phone, delete the fingerprint data that is currently stored and enroll a new fingerprint.
- Try clearing the cache partition on the device if the problem continues to occur.

It is expected that you will be able to restore the proper functionality of your fingerprint sensor if you follow these steps. It is recommended that you seek additional assistance if the problem continues to exist.

9. Samsung Galaxy S24 Ultra Crashing When Playing Games and Applications

It is a typical occurrence for users of both Android and iOS smartphones to experience sudden crashes of applications and games. Users of the Samsung Galaxy S24 Ultra have also reported experiencing this issue since the device's launch.

This problem often occurs when the device overheats, particularly when engaging in activities that are very strenuous, such as gaming.

The following are the steps that can be taken to solve the problem:

- Go to the **Settings menu** and look for the "Storage" option. Go inside and access both

"Cache" and "Data," then proceed to remove both of them.
- Try restarting your device.
- Make sure that the software version on your device is the most recent ever released.
- You should check for updates for your applications and install any updates that are available.
- It may be necessary to uninstall and then reinstall specific applications if they are the source of the problems.

You ought to be able to alleviate the crashing troubles that are occurring on your Samsung Galaxy S24 Ultra if you follow these procedures.

10. Problems with the Installation of Applications on Your Samsung Galaxy S24 Ultra.

Do you find that installing applications on your Samsung Galaxy S24 Ultra is somewhat tough for you? To solve the problem, proceed with the following steps:

Problems with the installation of applications on a Samsung S24 Ultra and how to fix them:

- Check to see if the application that you want to install is already installed on the device that you are using.
- To guarantee that installation from unknown sources is allowed, navigate to the **settings menu** and check the applicable box. Otherwise, you should turn on this option.
- Determine the amount of storage space available on your device; if it is already full, you can free up space by removing files that aren't necessary.
- After gaining access to the Google Play Store, navigate to its settings and turn off the **Play Protect feature.**

It is possible for you to install applications on your device without any problems if you follow these guidelines.

CONCLUSION

The Samsung S24 Ultra, the company's most recent flagship smartphone, is a resounding example of the highest level of innovation in the smartphone market. As one of the pioneers in this fusion, it attracts attention as a result of its combination of cutting-edge artificial intelligence technology and top-of-the-line hardware. The S24 Ultra is not only a premium device, but it also promises future-proofing with its adaptability to incoming AI-driven software updates. This makes it an appealing option for tech fans who are looking for the best. The S24 Ultra was designed to deliver an experience that is unsurpassed in its everyday use.

People who are always looking for the most recent technological improvements in smartphones will find the S24 Ultra to be an especially appealing option. Galaxy AI provides consumers with a glimpse into the future of mobile engagement by integrating its cutting-edge capabilities in a seamless manner into its operation. Furthermore, photography fans will find consolation in its amazing camera capabilities, which provide photographs of the greatest quality and come with editing features that are easy to use, guaranteeing that each and every snapshot is a beauty. An unrivaled gaming experience is provided by the S24 Ultra, which boasts a robust battery that enables gamers to enjoy extended gaming sessions without having to make any sacrifices.

When it comes down to it, the Samsung S24 Ultra emerges as the ideal option for consumers who are looking for a more advanced smartphone experience. In the smartphone market, this flagship device offers on all fronts, establishing a new bar for excellence. Whether you are a photography enthusiast, a passionate gamer, or someone who is intrigued by the possibilities of artificial intelligence integration, this device provides on all fronts.

ABOUT THE AUTHOR

Perry Hoover is a researcher, tech Entrepreneur, blogger and a technology writer, who is fond of blogging, technology research and writing. His areas of interest include Web application penetration testing, web security/architecture, cryptography, programming languages and database security. He is well versed with the latest technology, programming languages, computer hardware/software, and programming tools. He is also an expert in database security and application security architecture and penetration testing. He loves to share information about new technology and has published dozens of articles on it.

He has written articles on different aspects of IT Technologies including IT security, data storage and application development for magazines and has also published and co-published several e-books, of which the latest is on Windows 11. He has also worked with different private agencies to provide solutions to IT problems.

Printed in Great Britain
by Amazon

b0fe2293-83ba-4db1-a8fa-8607d68888abR01